Fierce Feminine Rising

"Never has such a book been so necessary or so timely for an endangered species—humanity. Our planet and all life on Earth are in peril. Now the voice of truth is screaming to be heard, and if we do not listen, we will become extinct. Explaining the falsities we have been fed as spiritual truth by the Dark Agenda, Anaiya Sophia exposes the lies by explaining just how such themes as 'we are all one' and 'it's all love' have deeper underlying meanings that must be faced and included for us to completely comprehend reality. She explains that we have been led to believe that we are facing the light, while we are actually searching for the light in abysmal darkness. In blazing terms, Anaiya Sophia describes the cultural overlay of misogynistic beliefs that have etched damaging patterns into our view of who we are. Calling for integrity, accountability, and honor, the feminine force as described by Anaiya Sophia invites us to annihilate our shared enemy of the Dark Agenda through fierce love for ourselves, for each other, and for our planet. Anaiya Sophia provides step-by-step guidelines in the last of her chapters for regaining our courage and choosing actions to clear us from past traumas and take the responsible and necessary steps to move forward into a balanced world. This may, per-haps, be one of the most important books ever written. It most certainly is a necessary read for all—women and men—who wish to deeply enter reality, change themselves, and help to create a better world."

PIA ORLEANE, PH.D., AUTHOR OF NAUTILUS GOLD AWARD–WINNING
SACRED RETREAT: USING NATURAL CYCLES TO RECHARGE YOUR LIFE

"The lioness fighting for her newborn cubs with every fiber of her life-giving power is fierce, tactical, uncompromising, and, yes, raging—for these desperate measures are her last resort. *This* is the wisdom and imperative behind *Fierce Feminine Rising,* where Anaiya Sophia will not shut her heart down to shadowy industries and governing forces that believe their misdeeds and malpractice against our beloved planet will go unchecked. And guess what? Mother Nature is on *her* side."

Linda Tucker, CEO of Global White Lion
Protection Trust and author of *Saving the White Lions*

"The 'real' Fierce Feminine lives life ablaze with shattering discrimination, deep passion, and heartfelt openness. Like a fiery phoenix, She is rising all around us. Anaiya Sophia's latest book captures a sliver of this fire, yet it's enough to set your whole existence aflame. Don't just read it—allow the wild love of the feminine to inspire you to sacred activism."

Andrew Harvey, author of *The Hope: A Guide to Sacred Activism*
and translator of *Turn Me to Gold: 108 Translations of Kabir*

"*Fierce Feminine Rising* is without doubt Anaiya Sophia's greatest work to date. Every generation has its way-showers, who navigate the fringes of consciousness and bring it to us all. This is what Anaiya does best—I've never read a body of work so alive and transformative as this. This is her game-changer."

James Twyman, New York Times
bestselling author and peace troubadour

"Any fierceness Anaiya possesses is always in service to the power of love and healing. This work is her passion and her calling, and this book is her masterpiece. She has pioneered the energy and message of the Fierce Feminine for the past two decades, and this book is arriving at the perfect time in our world and will help usher in the next wave of empowered feminine leadership."

Lee Harris, author of *Energy Speaks* and globally acclaimed
energy intuitive and transformation guide

"This is a galvanizing account of the Dark Feminine—passionate, wise, and necessary."

Jill M. Angelo, author of *Sacred Space:
Turning Your Home Into a Sanctuary*

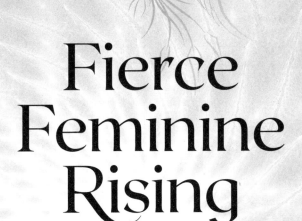

Fierce
Feminine
Rising

Heal from
Predatory Relationships &
Recenter Your Personal Power

ANAIYA SOPHIA

Destiny Books
Rochester, Vermont

Destiny Books
One Park Street
Rochester, Vermont 05767
www.DestinyBooks.com

Text stock is SFI certified

Destiny Books is a division of Inner Traditions International

Cataloging-in-Publication Data for this title is available from the Library of Congress

ISBN 978-1-62055-859-1 (print)
ISBN 978-1-62055-860-7 (ebook)

Printed and bound in the United States by Lake Book Manufacturing, Inc. The text stock is SFI certified. The Sustainable Forestry Initiative® program promotes sustainable forest management.

10 9 8 7 6 5 4 3 2 1

Text design by Priscilla H. Baker and layout by Virginia Scott Bowman
This book was typeset in Garamond Premier Pro and Avenir with Roxborough and Futura used as display typefaces

To send correspondence to the author of this book, mail a first-class letter to the author c/o Inner Traditions • Bear & Company, One Park Street, Rochester, VT 05767, and we will forward the communication, or contact the author directly at **anaiyasophia.com**.

Dedicated to my mother

The "New Age" is comfortable with the "conspiracy theories" that reveal the dangers of ecocide, fluoride, chemtrails, fracking, inorganic food and any other politically correct cause they can safely align within their Facebook profile without seeming too crazy. However, they are not ready to identify the core mutation that is causing these issues, and that is ultimately generating the systemic failure of their entire home planet . . . a genesis of bio-computational entropy that encompasses Humanity's true origins, history and the modification of its immortal blueprint.

JULIET CARTER

Contents

Take Me

You thought you were calling something beautiful—a goddess with sex-tossed hair and skin that glowed like the moon.

But you called La Loba. You called Baba Yaga. You called Inanna. You called Hecate. You called Pele. You called Kali Ma. You called the Crone.

You called the Dark Goddess to you.

She is the One that walks with sword and flame. Her face and hands are stained with blood and dirt. The earth shakes when she moves. The ocean swells.

You thought she would set you free. You thought she would give you power. You thought she would help you find something of yourself you lost.

Perhaps you did not know that first she would turn you to ash. First, she would have to destroy everything that you think you are.

And when she arrives, most who called her forth will run away in fear, they will take back their prayers and wish they had never seen her face.

Only a few will stop, turn towards her, and in that secret place of their heart, whisper,

"take me."

SEVAPREET

PREFACE
Rewilding the Feminine

FINALLY, ON THE WINTER SOLSTICE, She brought my fingers to the keyboard. "It's time to write," She announced. "On this night, we begin."

First, let me explain to you who "She" is. The She I'm referring to is the Fierce Feminine. The Fierce Feminine or Dark Mother is not a person, but instead our universal, individual, and collective expressed outrage. She is rising collectively now, especially within women, and has a unique and individual expression for each of us. We cannot truly grasp what this is unless we allow Her to authentically rise within us. This is the savage grace of the Fierce Feminine, as the true beauty of Her transmission is given only in authentic surrender.

When I first came upon this concept I wanted to know *what* the Fierce Feminine was, and why She was here now. Was this some kind of excuse for unleashing our own personal anger and resentment under the spiritual slogan of "sacred rage"? Or was this another feminist movement that publicly condemned all that is masculine and every man in the process? Despite all these questions, I knew there was a vital and necessary place for this energy in my own life. For too long I had pushed this great knowledge of injustice down for fear of what it might do, should it be spoken. I knew She existed; I could feel it in my bones. And so I began my quest to find Her and embody this authentic voice.

Try as I would, I was unable to write this book as I did my others. All my usual ways were rendered useless. For a start, I could only hear Her in the dark. If my mind was busy with planning, organizing, or sticking to a deadline, She fell silent. Only when I sank beneath the surface did I find Her. Her voice is there for all of us to hear, if only we are willing to silence our own.

As I was writing, She gave me strict guidelines on how this book was to be transcribed. She called this the "embodiment process." From what I understand, this process, this book, and everything within it is a living hologram. It is an *in the moment* experience. She wanted me to write as close to *the moment* as was humanly possible. I was unable to write anything if it was in the past; I could only write what was alive in the very now moment. She wanted me to write while it was still raw and partially formed, and to trust that. She wanted me to go through this unravelling process and to narrate my experiences. This kept me ever expanding, reaching for new words and ways to transcribe that which I did not know, and yet strangely did. She also requested a new language and a new way of transmitting knowledge. This, She told me, required a new and often unused part of the feminine brain, which She called "primordial wisdom." Primordial wisdom does not require learning, only living. It's simply here, as a vast resource of true being. It is our inner compass for what lies ahead.

The content She wants me to pass on to you was revealed during a series of sweaty and tumultuous dreams. For thirteen moons, during the last of my bleeding cycles, She exposed me to the velocity of Her transmission. These thirteen moons brought forth the thirteen chapters of this book, the foundation upon which Her message is revealed. She also asked for five spoken-word transmissions to be included in this body of work. That which cannot be written must be spoken. Those five transmissions can be downloaded at

audio.innertraditions.com/fiferi

and their transcripts are included in this book as noted in the table of contents.

Encoded within the oral transmissions is the gateway to gnosis, the direct contact with Her, where the continuation of Her mystery will take place long after this book has been closed. To really seal the deal, She asked me to reach into the depths of my heart to fetch the thirteen Sorrows of the World that I carry. These are the thirteen spears that pierce my heart and the thirteen rivers of grief that flow from them. I have peppered these sorrows throughout the book, placing them at the end of every chapter, so we never forget the purpose of the Fierce Feminine: to bring an end to these atrocities and the many more that you carry.

As far as I can see, She is using the seven forces of creation to lie the template upon. These seven forces are encoded into our psychospiritual bodies, also known as our chakra system. It's as if She is imbuing our centers of power with Her own. As this baton gets passed from Her to me and from me to you, Her permission and power soaks into our bones, birthing a new vocabulary that is laden with catalyzing codes that start to take shape and form, and will eventually be spoken.

She is attempting to entrust me/us with a process of unhooking from our deepest and most inauthentic behaviors. The purpose of this book is to serve as a transmission. Contained within these pages is a code, a frequency you have been waiting for. This frequency is the permission and power to speak up and speak out, and it's coming from Her to you. Should you allow this in, you'll be given your unique expression and cause to fully support.

From what I understand, the Fierce Feminine's mission is twofold. Not only does She intend to address and rebalance the powers that govern the planet by making sure every habitat has the right to thrive and that equilibrium is maintained, but also She will apply the same rigorous methods to fully balance and harmonize our own minds. Her journey is an inner and outer one. What we imagine is up ahead for the planet will be the same for our own brains. We will not be the spectators of this massive global cleanup campaign but participants ourselves. We can have this the easy way by surrendering to these truths, or we will experience it the hard way by resisting the inevitable and having it forced upon us.

Change is coming. Balance shall prevail.

Now let me introduce you to the Dark Agenda, otherwise known as the Matrix Control System. This includes the corrupt governments, the war-making industries, the overproducing, mind-numbing, addiction-feeding, heartlessness of our modern-day society, as well as the covert influences of anti-awakening that seem to be taking advantage of our digital technology to spread their virus. This Dark Agenda has always been here, but it has come into its own since the First World War. From that time, the families, or rather the bloodlines, started to work together as a cartel to dominate the world economy and prevent the full realization of our spiritual and abundant nature.

This is precisely Her concern and the main thrust of Her message. She is rising within us to initiate the full-on realization of how vulnerable and fragile the whole human race and a great deal of nature are at this extremely dangerous moment in history. I believe the Fierce Feminine is giving us one last chance to be here. It's time to "know thyself" and rise up, as herstory could be different, if only we listen and respond right away. I feel She will first speak to us creatively and spiritually by drawing us in with Her vision and innovation. She will then show us what's possible, and what will happen if we ignore Her. If we accept Her ideas and creations, She will flush out the patriarchal contamination from our minds. The journey will be scary, but it will be fully supported. If we do not accept the Fierce Feminine's offer to stay here, as a true ambassador of what She originally intended for humankind, then I believe we may well be facing extinction.

It's important to clarify here that the problem is not only "out there" but also within. The corruption that we see in every city, every country, and every government has an invisible counterpart controlling our own minds. So beloved friends, we're going down deep into that rabbit hole to set ourselves free. We're going to address what has been hidden from our view since the beginning of time. This book is not only the call for sacred activism in the world, but spiritual activism—in every moment.

I truly believe that the Fierce Feminine is humanity's last and only hope.

—*Anaiya Sophia*

Acknowledgments

There are so many people I would like to acknowledge who helped during the process of writing *Fierce Feminine Rising*. It has taken a true collaboration of events, challenges, unexpected allies, and tremendous faith to birth this body of work.

First, I would like to acknowledge my parents, Dinah and Patrick Cuddihy, who gave me the nickname She Who Must Be Obeyed as I grew up. I now realize they were absolutely right!

I would like to acknowledge my totally switched-on editor, Kristian Strang, who worked brilliantly with Her words and strange ways of slinging together a sentence. True teamwork Kristian!

I would like to acknowledge my inspirational friend Gertrud Keazor for awakening me to a new dawn in terms of fierceness. What a revelation! Thank you, Sweedy!

I would like to acknowledge Jon Graham, Kelly Bowen, Patricia Rydle, Meghan MacLean, Jill Rogers, Manzanita Carpenter, and the team at Inner Traditions, who supported and strongly encouraged the birth of this book during a time of tremendous personal challenge and insisted upon its expansion. Thank you for publishing this work and continuing to support my voice out in the world.

I would like to acknowledge the brilliant, pioneering, penetrating, glittering stars of the written word, who have kindly gifted me the privilege of including their voices in this book. They are: Anne Baring, Christopher Wallace, Zola Dubnikova, Lisa Renee, Bernhard Guenther,

Sevapreet Hesser, Jessica Davidson, Heidi Klob, Juliet Carter, and Linda Tucker.

Thank you also to Andrew Harvey for his unprecedented inspiration, outspokenness, tenderness, and action. You have been and are a tremendous guide for me.

Finally, I would like to acknowledge my solid, dependable, and trusted husband, Pete Wilson, for his endless support and infinite patience and for having my back in times of trial. There is no possibility of being able to do, be, say, or write anything without knowing in the deepest part of my bones that we are in this together. I love and respect you so deeply.

To all who read this book and take its message to heart: Thank you for feeling our plight!

—*Anaiya Sophia*

Part One

Introduction
to the
Fierce Feminine

ONE
What *Is* the Fierce Feminine (and What *Is Not*)?

AS PROMISED, THE PROCESS OF WRITING *Fierce Feminine Rising* orchestrated a perfect set of circumstances for me to not only find Her authentic voice but to be willing and daring enough to speak it out. Running parallel alongside my creative endeavors was a series of real-life events that called for the zero-tolerance attitude of the Fierce Feminine.

I found myself speaking out publicly to warn others about a dangerous predator in our spiritual community. In response, he threatened me for defaming his character, demanding a ridiculous amount of money to compensate for his loss of earnings. I roared back that defamation is not defamation when what has been written is true. I let him know that he would have to prove my words were untrue in a court of law, which would, of course, be impossible. I then roared at the legal firm he used, letting them know that if I was to receive another letter written to me in this same manner that I would report their threatening, accusatory misconduct and unprofessionalism to the police.

Weeks later I found myself in another situation where the health of a very dear friend was deteriorating rapidly. He was being taken care of in a way that his family was not happy with. Once again, the Fierce Feminine's passion for doing the right thing rose within me, and I found myself stepping into an extremely charged and delicate situation, insisting upon an action where the good care of our friend was of paramount importance. I again spoke up, whereas years ago I would have been shuffling my feet, looking at the ground, hoping someone else would take charge.

In the dark nights of winter, She had foretold this; in the early days of spring, I was stepping into my power and speaking on Her behalf.

By allowing this new way to be creative, listening to Her wisdom and accurately following Her suggestions, my life changed dramatically. What I noticed and must enthusiastically share is how quickly the process ignited. Once I said yes to Her call and followed this with regular journaling and deep listening, and then spoke to those around and within me—without editing Her voice—I was on a roller coaster of a ride.

Allowing the Fierce Feminine to have Her voice creates a lot of waves and surprises! We must realize that by speaking Her voice, we will be challenging the core of those around us. The Fierce Feminine has this ability to get past defenses and strike at the nervous systems of those holding old positions of power or false goodness. Like a powerful young horse who has been released from the quiet confines of the paddock, we must give Her her head. We must let Her go—speak freely, choose wisely, act steadfastly, and initiate the things we never would have dreamt of doing before.

But how do we know if this is the Divine will of the Fierce Feminine and not our own personal anger looking for a fight? Well, I believe there's a hallmark; a clear and easy-to-spot situation that marks Her good works as Her own. When we speak and act on behalf of the Fierce Feminine, it will most likely have nothing to do with our own personal gain. The situation and the reason why we're speaking out will be on behalf of those who cannot. I believe it to be that clean of an energy. And should we find ourselves in a place that requires defense and protection of our own Light, it will be because that position defends others—many, many others at the same time.

When we allow the justice of the Fierce Feminine to flow within us, we will feel it in our hearts that we're doing the right thing. There will be a buoyant upsurge of courageous goodness, like a victory cry that rallies tremendous resources and resilience. When She speaks it feels clean and triumphant. There's no venom, no vitriol, and no rhetoric. When you let go, there is no argument, no fight, and no conflict—there is only Truth. There may be a denial of that Truth, but the usual way that humans solve their differences—via fighting—does not happen. The Fierce Feminine does not enter the fight. She is working on and in realms where physical brawling is a thing of the past.

In the times I have allowed the Fierce Feminine Her head, She has put me in contact with a third and unknown power that is neither good nor bad. It just *is*. This part of me can see all sides of the situation quickly. Even before everyone has stated their positions, it's clear to me who stands where. I can see the bullshit, the tactics deployed, the lies, the hidden emotion, and a sense of what's not being said. Without thought, a swift and direct action, voice, or response emerges. The narrow window of possible outcomes from my own narrative on life melts down in surrender as a brilliant flash of response is born.

This enlivening experience of an altered state of reality restores and recalibrates when we give of ourselves on Her behalf. And that is the Truth. We take a leap of faith on Her behalf, and simultaneously, She powers Herself through our being, birthing within us a wholly new operating system.

As exciting and wonderful as this sounds, we will most likely get met by resistance and angry accusations from those that we challenge. This is to be expected, so there's no need to worry. All we do is ground ourselves in Her beingness and do our best not to take any of it personally. We must remember: it's not so much a person that opposes us, but a system; a heavy, deeply enmeshed, dense way of living alongside old values, old beliefs, and old ideas. That's what we're challenging, and that's why there will be tremendous resistance. But if we know that in advance, we will be prepared and ready for it.

The lists on the following page provide characteristics that describe what the Fierce Feminine is, and what the Fierce Feminine is not.

What *Is* the Fierce Feminine?

- Showing courage
- Seeking truth
- Acting on behalf of the innocent and undefended
- Responding effectively
- Being willing to speak up and speak out
- Protecting your Light and the Light of others
- Taking a stand
- Being fully aware of visible and invisible situations
- Inwardly praying for true alignment and blessings for the situation
- Walking away feeling you acted on Her behalf
- Feeling restored and recalibrated by your actions

What Is *Not* the Fierce Feminine?

- Displaying false bravado
- Telling lies
- Acting from self-interest and personal gain
- Reacting and causing a scene
- Employing passive-aggressive tactics to coerce, blame, and attack
- Attacking the Light of others
- Being defiant and stubborn
- Losing awareness of the whole situation
- Inwardly building more aggression
- Walking away, plotting another attack
- Feeling agitated and restless by your actions

I believe we all have an urgent quest that has been waiting an incredibly long time for us to accept. Every single one of us has a piece of the puzzle that we must contribute to the community we are a part of. To do that, I suspect we will have to reach beyond our comfort zones and into the unknown to pull through a new level of consciousness that we sense in our gut as our own. She is wanting to speak to the world. No one person can do this on Her behalf, yet we can make our own sound. The more we utter Her sounds, the quicker Her transmission can form. Her voice cannot be spoken through a human language; nor can it be written or read. Perhaps what I'm sensing is a frequency of harmonic aliveness that mirrors Her own. A new way of being here that not only bestows peace on Earth but takes us forward into another creation story—this time fully conscious and participating bravely. I sense in return, She graces us with a new method of communication, if only we could do away with the old. Not only does this new way open deeper and more mystical sections of the brain but also the impulse to speak from them.

This is a radical and amazing time that we are living in. And now, in this the eleventh hour, not only is the Divine Feminine offering us one last chance to be here but also the opportunity to make a vast and quantum leap in our whole society. But it will have to be on Her terms.

Yulin Dog Meat Festival

Yulin, a city in the Guangxi province of China, is home to a "festival" that takes place on June 21 of every year during the summer solstice and lasts for ten long, horrifying days in which 10,000 to 15,000 dogs (as well as cats) are tortured and then consumed. However, it's estimated that up to 25 million dogs are stolen, sold, bought, and eaten every year within the illegal dog and cat meat trade.* A larger percentage of these dogs consist of pets stolen from their families. The rest of the dogs are captured strays from the streets and some are even raised in dog farms. After these animals are stolen, bought, or captured they are then transported for days without any food or water, crammed together in tiny cages so tightly that they are unable to move.

*Statistical information from the Stop Animal Cruelty in Yulin website, https://stop-animal-cruelty-in-yulin-84.webself.net/accueil.

Throughout the festival, these animals are hung, burned, skinned, boiled, torched, dismembered, electrocuted, and beaten—often *alive* and out in the streets for public view. But if that isn't bad enough, they intentionally torture these animals in front of the other animals to create more stress and fear. The reason behind torturing and slaughtering the animals while they're still *alive* is that the people of Yulin believe that the more adrenaline and fear that runs through the animals' blood, the more tender and better tasting the meat will be.

Animal rights advocate and actor Ricky Gervais took to social media on this issue to share his views on this controversial festival: "It's sadistic, it's fucking mental," a visibly upset Gervais began. "It's like hell. It's the fucking nastiest thing I've ever heard of . . . I am at a loss."

Since dogs are considered companion animals in Europe and the United States, seeing them suffer in this way strikes deeply at us all. Especially since some of the dogs that have been rescued from the meat trade were found to have microchips in them, sometimes even collars! I can't even imagine the pain that some must feel from not only getting their dogs stolen but knowing of the horrible fate that lies before them.

Together, as a society, we can put an end to this madness. We cannot sit idly and let these things sort themselves out on their own. And every day that we remain silent is another day we have decided that these animals are not worth the fight. If you want to join the movement to end the Yulin Dog Meat Festival, please sign the Humane Society International's petition, and please consider donating to the cause as well. You can sign the petition and donate on the Dog Meat Trade page on the Humane Society International's website.

Pause here for reflection. Take the time needed to truly be with these insights and understandings. Just breathe and be with them. Let's bear witness to the sobriety of the situation and feel one another as we rise together to receive more of Her transmission.

Let's move on without answers.

We must learn to trust the process, remembering that *this is an initiation.*

TWO
Seven Ways to Ignite Our Fierce Feminine

IN THE BEGINNING . . . I WAS WILD AND UNRULY, creative, and fun! I was free to speak and free to love. Free to show outrage and brave enough to challenge it . . . I wish I could say that I was all those things, but I wasn't. I was born shy, often alone, and eager to please. I believe I silently agreed to take on all of this while in the womb. Like a slow-motion passing of the baton, I took from my mother and father that which they were unable to become. And by the time I was born, I fitted in perfectly to a world of fence-sitting, armchair-watching viewers of wrongness.

I was a pale imitation of what my Soul ached to live. I could feel the "No!" well up inside of me but dared not scream it. There were a couple of times when it spontaneously erupted—and I was immediately chastised. All in all, I learned quickly that fighting the good fight was not allowed. This realization dampened down the compassionate fire and turned it into inner anger. Within that smoldering humiliation my connection to who I really was hung by a diminishing thread as the memory of I AM was almost forgotten.

It wasn't until I got married, or rather divorced, when things began to melt down and change for me. People who knew me back then would say it was a sweet and smiley angel that descended into the hellhole of that marriage, and God knows it was a wild woman that clawed herself back out. With dirt under my broken fingernails and tangled and matted hair, I started to piece myself back together. My mask was in tatters on the floor, as my false persona was ripped from me. All the outrages began to bubble to the surface gasping for air. I was breaking free of so much, only I didn't know it at the time.

In the quiet and unseen dark, She sang over my bones, bringing me back to life. She had pulled me from the clutches of the Dark Agenda and kept vigil as I wrestled with the demons who came to pull me back. She knew I wasn't going back—but I didn't. Everything seemed real and believable. But She was not fazed. She knew that I had undergone a terrible initiation, one I had insisted upon. And keeping true to Her word, She airlifted me out the moment I was ready. We both knew that one day I would rise with a power and presence that would shake the world. We both knew that I, and others, would unite across the world on Her behalf and roar "No more!" to everything that opposed Her vision. Like the bionic woman, She remade me in Her image until I realized that She . . . was me.

My story is Herstory. And it's being written as we read.

She is reaching into every life of those who are ready, willing, and able to surrender to Her vison and imbuing them with Her ferocity. She does not bow down to societal demands and expectations, as She has Her own moral code. She is here to free people, animals, and the planet from the onslaught of greed, control, and disregard that has enslaved it. Her alchemy shall take place in both the outer and inner worlds, and Her intention is to uproot, dislodge, and clean all of Her Creation.

It's essential that this Fierce Feminine force is given the space She requires to complete the purpose She has been called upon to do. For too long the Dark Agenda has slowly crept under our skin. Pulling us from the natural world and into their hybrid mutation. But of course, we like it—in fact we love it! It's bright and shiny and gives us status and power and good feelings . . . for a while anyway. And then it takes us down, like a dark crocodile, into the black waters where we cannot breathe or rise to the surface again. She, the Fierce Feminine, looks on with intensity. She does not want us silenced or bound any longer. The molten core of Her heart has become filled with the years we've been imagining everything is okay. It isn't. The Dark Agenda has created a death machine that doesn't know how to stop. We have become a species out of control. There are too many of us and still we keep multiplying! We use energy to create more than we need, and we use energy to get rid of what has been created. Why we don't give our overproduction to those in need is beyond me. Although I suppose it's not profitable to do so.

If we carry on like this, there will be no more planet. The reality is that we may become extinct and take a large chunk of nature with us.

Together we are facing the death machine as an opposing and immense power that threatens total annihilation. She is the force that will end it, either way. She cries out to anyone listening to prepare for a possible new future and to joyfully live out our last years, leaving the planet better off than when we came to it.

We must know that it's now two minutes to midnight, and She is offering us one last chance. In an act of uncompromising mercy, She holds out Her hand, bringing us the wisdom to cut through the sleep state of the Dark Agenda, with its denial and illusion, and help birth a new future for us all. The only catch is this: the moment you touch Her hand you are infused with a quickening that is translated through you into action. She offers a unique and individual embodiment process that must not be blocked, or it will become lost.

As I began to tune in to Her presence, knowing that I had chosen to write this book, She sent me on a journey. Within days of creating an altar to the Fierce Feminine, a wild and unruly energy emerged that not only revealed but pried me away from the false agreements I had been making with the world. It was staggering to see and shocking to experience. She showed me that the seven psychospiritual centers (chakras) in every human being needed to be hoisted up in vibration to a resonance beyond interference from the Dark Agenda. Every day I would turn to Her presence, which seemed to overlay a template within me. I began to feel this new resonance as my own. By communing with Her, I was becoming Her. I was beginning to see—Her message is energy.

Everything about the Fierce Feminine is resonance, vibration, and frequency. By allowing Her energy and template into our awareness and cells, we can unhook ourselves from the Dark Agenda. But we will have to pull each and every single one of those cords from the seven chakras that's embedded into the Dark Agenda ourselves and place them in Her hands. Although this seems like a big deal, it actually isn't. All it takes is vigilance and desire. We must want it.

We have a choice, beloved friends. Either we accept and live by Her new template, and thereby become part of the new creation, or we shall diminish our own existence by allowing the death machine to run its course. It has never been clearer for me. I have never dared to inquire into the subjects that fill these pages before now. And I can see that the transformation that is needed is reachable, but it will take all of our awareness to attain it. And this is the win-win situation, because in the process of doing this, we get our own minds back.

For the remainder of this chapter, we're going to glance over the template that awakens our Fierce Feminine and, no doubt, be confronted with the ways we have silenced Her. As we progress deeper into this book, every turning of the page will draw the attention of Her force into these areas for a lasting and genuine change within you. The more you read, the more you will summon Her up and into your life.

One last thing I must mention before moving forward. She would always use inclusive terminology when speaking with and through me. She only ever gave me the impression of we, our, us. It was never *you* or *I*. For example, She would hint, "We need to stand our ground," and I would sense that She meant me, you, and Her. It was never, "You need to stand your ground." She never told me what to do, but rather what we had to become.

We are about to go on an authentic journey. So let's begin at the beginning and work from the ground up.

STANDING OUR GROUND

There is a sickness within humanity today, a deep suppression of our interconnectivity as the powers that be, or Dark Agenda, continually attempt to segregate, separate, and stagnate our natural tendencies to share and pass on our wisdom. This false way of living keeps us flighty, flaky, and unable to manifest our sacred gifts. We then become disconnected, disenchanted, and disloyal to ourselves and to all that has been given to us. To remedy this sickness, we must burst out of the cages that isolate us and get connected to the causes and concerns that break our hearts wide open. We can no longer waste time; instead we must find our tribe, find our location, and settle down to the task at hand by becoming trustworthy guardians of our local domain.

It's time to sink down into our roots and reconnect with the natural, the primal, and the instinctual. It's time to untether and reclaim all the aspects of ourselves that have been shamed, hidden, and tamped down so we can ground our full being and powerful medicine into the world. We must dig extra deep and restore the sacred gift and wisdom that's been placed in our being, for exactly this time. We each have an evolutionary gift to bring to the table that will take courage to find and conviction to share. But we must if we are to stand as She—unapologetic, unashamed, and unmoving. We must pass on our wisdom, and inform, inspire, and illuminate. We must gather the people, create the space, and make it happen.

Our very lives and the well-being of humanity depend on it now.

We need to stand our ground and pass on our wisdom.

SOVEREIGN SEXUALITY

According to the highest tantric texts and the sacred wisdom being remembered by priestesses today, the sexual act is not only the most potent transformational medicine, it is also the hidden doorway to unprecedented awakening. Sexual alchemy is the transformation of our dense nature into something more refined and pure, if we create the sacred space for Her to enter.

Like the symbol of the cross, there is the vertical mark that symbolizes the masculine plane out into the cosmos and the horizontal mark that symbolizes the feminine plane out into the world. When we bring these two together in ourselves, and with another, we create the rigorous life energy and depth of being that we so need. This sacred infusion of aliveness will bless our bodies, minds, and hearts with the endurance and stamina needed to keep on keeping on during these tumultuous times.

It's time to sink into our genitals and stop wasting our energy on mindless sex that is goal-oriented or plugged into the pornographic world. These human tendencies have been monopolized by an extremely dark force, what we are calling the Dark Agenda, that ensnares our vital life force, creating a powerful addiction that snuffs out the beckoning doorway to this vast awakening and intimacy with another. This is precisely what the Dark Agenda wants: addictive, sniveling wretches unable to see or care about what is going on around them—mere sexual junkies.

To counter this, we must only say yes to those moments that will replenish us, elevate us, and bring us genuinely closer together.

The very power that could set us on fire must not be dampened down by compromise.

We need to reclaim and elevate our sovereign sexuality.

ACCOUNTABILITY, BOUNDARIES, AND INTEGRITY

It's time to apply the Fierce Feminine to the realm of boundaries, standing up and saying no to the energetic drains, the distractions, and the constant onslaught of social media and the never-ending to-do list. All of this weakens our will and is brilliantly designed to do so. We are being urged to look at our wishy-washy choices, half-hearted decisions, and feelings of entitlement and scream out, "No more!" Instead, let us tap into the energy of rebellion and the sacred rebel within us. Be the resister to all that is false and untrue.

We have to honestly check in with ourselves and ask, "Am I walking the path that I claim to be? Am I still squandering piles of money, time, and energy on superficial materialism and unnecessary travel? How do I get rid of that which I no longer need?"

Accountability, integrity, and honor are the qualities that smash to smithereens the doctrines of the Dark Agenda that are forced upon us. We must remember there are right and wrong actions in this world, and we must be willing to be one who steps into right living and right actions.

The Fierce Feminine is hunting for people who are willing to stand up and say, "No, not on my watch am I going to let you take away the basic human rights and dignity of my brothers and sisters." She needs men and women to stand up and bring the daily cruel and barbaric horrors to an end. Every day animals, nature, and people are forced to give up their bodies, land, and time in an attempt to feed the insane hunger of an overpopulated world. In truth, the only entitlement we have is to share the resources that are mindfully given.

No one is more deserving than another.

We must not compromise our personal integrity.

DISCERNMENT, DEPTH, AND AWAKENING IN RELATIONSHIPS

Relationships take on a whole new level for anyone who has chosen to embody the Fierce Feminine, i.e., anyone who is sincerely engaged in seeking truth, speaking out, and deprogramming others from the current cultural/social norms to transcend the Dark Agenda.

A relationship with another who has taken the "red pill" as it were (as seen in the movie *The Matrix*) provides the crucible for genuine and amplified transformation. However, you could also find yourself careening head and heart first into all kinds of strange and menacing territories. This is where discernment comes in, as well as the ability to be aware and speak up. It takes courage to speak out against the tide of popular opinion. And that's exactly what we must do—we must speak out, love more, humble ourselves often, tell the truth, show up, go out on a limb, defend the innocent, and trust our intuition.

Courage is the ability to do something that frightens you. This means that you don't get away from feeling the fear or even being trampled by it. But when you can, you rise and stand as She does—ready, willing, and able to do what must be done.

For too long we have stayed in abusive relationships, denied the amount of debt we are in, turned our back on cruel behavior, protected the industries we have worked for, defended the country we were born into, and hidden the many ways in which our hearts are broken. It is time to not live up to the expectations placed upon us. It's time to disregard other people's opinions and to live by our own moral compass.

Again, society has been rendered useless under the spell of "what other people might think." This creates a status quo held in place by false means. I suggest we examine carefully all that we are agreeing to quite simply because we are too afraid to challenge it.

A yes is a yes. A no is a no. And an "I don't know" is also a no.

We must take heart and be brave.

BREAKING OUR SILENCE

Spiritual awakening and self-actualization are no longer a luxury; they're an imperative. Because of our collective level of access, privilege, and opportunity, we must be a moral and awake force on this planet, continually transforming the world into a better place.

One of the ways in which we sabotage our brilliance and effectiveness is by not telling the truth. Lies, secrets, and cover-ups create the weight of guilt upon our shoulders, dulling down our beauty and spontaneity and giving rise to anger. Guilt is once again an energy that the

Dark Agenda loves to play with. It pulls us here, there, and everywhere as the whole artificial world is created by the pursuit of pleasure and the avoidance of guilt, leaving us feeling like rudderless ships upon the ocean.

The only way out of this quagmire is to tell the truth—the absolute and relative truth. We must wield the sword of discernment, cutting through denial and illusion until we find the pure and untainted Truth. And yes, this feels dangerous—because it is. We fear we will lose something if we reveal it. So we stay silent. But we cannot carry on this way any longer.

We must light up like a meteor and access our sacred rage as we excavate our throats in search of our authentic voice. Let us create safe containers where we can access these deep-down voices and encourage one another to sound them with full authenticity. Over time our one voice will join with many others to become a unified sound of (r)evolution.

Our sacred rage is the catalyzing agent of change.

We must not be silent when truth needs to be spoken.

SHE WHO KNOWS

This terrestrial, human world is constantly invaded by the forces of the neighboring world, that is, of the vital world, the subtler region beyond the Earth's atmosphere and our five senses. This vital world is constantly penetrating the physical world and is much more subtle. It's often quite imperceptible except to a few rare individuals.

There are entities, beings, wills, and various types of individualities in that world who have all kinds of intentions and make use of every opportunity to either amuse themselves, if they are small beings, or to do harm and create disorder, if they are beings with a greater capacity. Over the millennia we have been drip-fed a junkie fix of distractions and dumbing-down agents to keep us from knowing what we have every right to know.

We have tamed ourselves, kept ourselves small, and often ignored our pure knowing for fear of being harmed, judged, tortured, shamed, and killed because of it. No wonder it is so hard to trust in ourselves again. But that's exactly what we must now do.

She will speak to us through this feminine channel. By those with the ears to hear is Her voice heard. And this is her rehabilitation process. By trusting in ourselves, we hear Her voice. By listening to Her, our trust is restored. That is the medicine of the Fierce Feminine.

Trust and intuition go hand in hand, and each feeds the other. Surrender your masculine mind and its insistent need for proof, logic, and clear thinking. Instead, delve deep into the animal nature of your being, and sniff, snuffle, track, and scan. Everything you need to know is within you.

Remember, Her channel is wisdom, discernment, knowing, and a pure sense of doing the right thing. To restore our intuition, we will have to overthrow the Dark Agenda's sedation. Lifting one veil at a time, we shall start to see things (and people) as they truly are. She will reveal to us a way to live in harmony with the natural world and its natural inhabitants. The fallout, however, will be the acute ability to see that which is unnatural, artificial, and "watching our every move." We won't be able to say we don't know anymore. These forces have a vested interest in maintaining the Dark Agenda, and they will go to extraordinary lengths to suppress any destabilizing factors that could disrupt their food supply.

This is the price tag for knowing thyself.

We must trust our intuition and see things as they really are.

ORIGINAL INNOCENCE

These days most of us are in survival mode, our nervous systems continually activated by the horrors being inflicted on people, places, and animals across the globe. This is unsustainable, so we must find ways to nurture and come home to ourselves.

All of the crises of our time are variations on the theme of separation and ignorance. Until we awaken to our origins, the deep wellspring of our essential nature, we will not flourish. In these chaotic times, we need a spiritual resource to ground us so we can stay centered in our sacred work and do what truly matters each day. We need to lean into the spiritual technology and sustenance contained within ritual, prayer, and ceremony to galvanize our personal resources.

However, we must be mindful of a trap that's out there: the false teachers, communities, and religions that entice us to their door. They offer not faith, but fear. They take the precious stirrings of our Soul and misuse the trust (and money) we have placed in them. We must be vigilant and trust our intuition, and should we suspect we are in the grip of a false guru, leave immediately. The level of damage can be immense and extremely dangerous. The effects of being under the influence of a false guru or rehabilitating afterward is the astonishing amount of time it takes to heal, or not. The deepest levels of trust have been compromised, and it takes a gallant Soul to learn to open up again. The aftermath can stay with a person for the rest of their lives. In some circles this kind of wounding is known as a psychic scar, a permanent dent in the texture of the Soul that must at some stage become the very feature that illuminates the corrupt foulplay.

Cultivating awakening is a vulnerable process, and it must be treated with reverence and care. The great work of the Soul is to gather all the divergent parts together and forge them into an undivided unity. The only other person who could possibly walk this journey with us is someone sincerely on the path, or someone a little farther ahead. The hallmarks of being ahead can only be compassion, joy, and encouragement. Manipulation, accusation, judgment, fear, superiority, and arrogance are dead giveaways that your guide is a masquerader. Your spiritual guide is only there to serve your authentic awakening and to remind you of the power of who you are, including the power of your discernment.

Our original innocence is a precious and sacred fire that burns within. We must enshrine its purity within our hearts. We shall go into great depth on this subject throughout our time together in this book.

Our original innocence is the crown we once lost.

❦

The Fierce Feminine is the medicine we most hunger for in this moment of our evolution, but we may not know it. We are sick and tired of stasis, remaining the same, and not getting anywhere.

This longed-for force shall open us to gnosis, revelation, and wild ecstatic freedom. Many people hold back, fearing Her ferociousness will tip them over the edge, and they will become too wild, too mad and unpredictable. This is the voice of fear that will always keep you from Her.

The Fierce Feminine will loosen our minds, shake off our masks, vivify our sacred purpose, and make real our Soul essence and reason for being here. As we come into contact with this forbidden part of ourselves, this long-awaited union explodes the body, heart, and mind into a third, and currently unknown, being. Something the Dark Agenda has feared for an incredibly long time, but She—and we—have patiently longed for.

> *In the middle of my life I suddenly awoke*
> *and found myself in a wood so dark that the road was*
>   *wholly lost.*
> *So cruel and lightless was this wood that I can hardly*
>   *speak of it,*
> *mere memory stirs such terror in my blood,*
> *that even now I feel I am about to die.*
> *Yet in that place I found such great and unexpected good*
> *that I will tell the tale and all I saw therein.*
>   DANTE'S *INFERNO*

Pig Farming

The film *Land of Hope and Glory* shows the truth of the animal "farming" industry in the United Kingdom. The film begins by recognizing the picture the marketing world paints of farms: picturesque rural landscape, happily roaming animals, and serenity. The picture that comes to mind when most of us think of farmland and farm animals. It goes on to acknowledge that the reality of farming in the United Kingdom (and we could extend this to the world in general) is the opposite of this and that consumers are lulled into feeling good about their meat purchases by clever advertising and sneaky branding—including organic, free-range, high-welfare, and SPCA-approved. This film encourages us to open our eyes to the truth and to make conscious changes based on that truth.

Following is some of the poignant information about pig farming shared in that film; you can watch the full film on the Land of Hope and Glory website.

On [UK] farms the pigs receive no care and compassion and are treated as no more than objects, classified as "property." There is no beauty on a pig farm . . . it is a production line that takes these animals from birth to death. . . .

Only 3 percent of pigs will spend their entire lives outdoors. . . . Most pigs are officially entitled to less than one square meter of space each and the majority of sows, or female breeding pigs, are kept in farrowing crates . . . . These crates are so small that the sows cannot turn around in them and the mother pigs are forced to stay in these crates for up to five weeks at a time, every time they give birth.

The majority of sows in the UK are artificially inseminated in order to ensure they are continuously pregnant. This cycle of forced impregnation and confinement is repeated over and over again for about three to five years or until the sow is too exhausted to carry on. At this point, she is then slaughtered for low-grade meat such as pies, pasties, and sausage meat. There is often no bedding and no sewage system on the farms, which causes excrement to pile up underneath and around the pigs, forcing them to lay in their own feces for weeks on end, creating the perfect environment for diseases and infection to thrive. . . .

In the wild, piglets would remain with their mothers for around twelve to fourteen weeks. But in UK farms, piglets are taken away from their mothers after only three to four weeks. . . . Farmers also inflict horrific mutilations on piglets by amputating their tails and clipping their teeth. All of which is done without anaesthetic or painkillers. . . . If the piglets are not growing fast enough or are sick and injured, they are seen as unprofitable to the industry so are then killed. This is done in the most cost effective manner, meaning that often the piglets are slammed against walls, concrete floors, or bludgeoned with metal poles. . . .

Across the country countless pig farm workers have been documented torturing, maiming, and beating pigs. Consequently many pigs carry open wounds and deep lacerations and many die before making it to the slaughterhouse.

When the pigs reach slaughter age at around six months, they're transported in cramped and overcrowded trucks with no food or water. After undergoing extremely traumatic journeys they are shown no mercy and are herded to their deaths. . . .

One of the methods of slaughter for pigs in the UK is the gas chamber, where groups of pigs are herded into metal cages, which are then dropped into a chamber that is filled with carbon dioxide. Once inside the chamber, the pigs scream and thrash, fighting for their lives for up to 30 seconds. This method of slaughter is used for UK supermarkets including Tesco, Asda, Sainsbury's, Lidl, and Waitrose.

The other certified humane method of pig slaughter in the UK is electrical stunning with the aim to render the animals unconscious before they have their throats slit. However, stunning is often poorly executed by rushed slaughterhouse workers, which results in an estimated 1.8 million pigs regaining consciousness at the production line each year and being fully conscious as they die from blood loss.*

I know it's hard, but if you can, please sit through this film and allow yourself to feel, witness, and authentically respond. Please, don't turn away from what is happening. The earth, these pigs, all those who are suffering, need to be witnessed and comforted by our grief.

Pause here for reflection. Take the time that is needed to truly be with these insights and understandings. Just breathe and be with them. Let's bear witness to the sobriety of the situation and feel one another as we rise together to receive more of Her transmission.

Let's move on without answers.

We must learn to trust the process, remembering that *this is an initiation.*

Land of Hope and Glory, created by the founders of animal rights organization Surge with research and editing done by Ed Winters and Luna Woods, 2017, Land of Hope and Glory: UK Animal Farming website. You can find a full list of the public investigations featured in the film on the website as well as additional facts and references.

THREE
War on Consciousness
How to Deal with the Soul's Predator

IF YOU THINK THE HUMAN PSYCHE IS COMPOSED primarily of decency and light, you might want to skip this chapter. For here we shall plunge into a reality that is difficult to comprehend: the world of "evil." As terrifying and unacceptable as it might seem, we must realize that there are predators, out there and within us, that are anti-life and full of darkness. Here's how Jungian analyst Heidi Kolb explains it in her blog post about the Bluebeard fairy tale:

> There is an innate predator and killer in psyche. A psychic force that cannot be "rehabilitated." A psychic force that does not transform. The challenge with all archetypal energies is to learn how to relate to them without being overtaken. For the feminine psyche, which always wants to connect and relate, this anti-life force is probably the most difficult one to come to terms with. It is too much for an individual psyche to digest.*

I truly believe this is precisely what the Fierce Feminine gives us— the courage and steadfastness to endure what we must endure to become

---

*Excerpt from Heidi Kolb, "Bluebeard ~ A Killer to Reckon With: How to Survive the Soul's Predator," Heidikolb's Blog, September 18, 2010. Used with permission from Heidi M. Kolb, Jungian analyst.

free. It is precisely here, in this subject where the mind is most enslaved and too afraid to face. Heidi goes on to say that

> the mythical imagination has always produced images and stories of this psychic reality. The tale of Bluebeard is one of them. Fairy tales are simple and pure expressions of the collective unconscious and offer a clear understanding of universal patterns in the human psyche. . . .
>
> Just like a dream, a fairy tale is not to be taken literally. It depicts the dance and the dynamics between the two grand archetypal forces, the masculine and the feminine, as they manifest in the collective as well as in the individual psyche. Both dreams and fairy tales can be a roadmap to discern an attitude that will allow, in fairy tale terms, for the princess to get her prince, and in Jungian language, for the union of opposites and the sacred marriage of the masculine and the feminine within one's soul.*

THE STORY OF BLUEBEARD

This is the story of Bluebeard as told by Jessica Davidson on her blog.

> Once there was a man with a strange blue beard who, as luck would have it, was called Bluebeard. It was said he was a failed magician, but he didn't like to talk about it. Instead, he concentrated all his efforts on procuring a new wife and courted three sisters at the same time. He took them on a lavish picnic and impressed them with tales of his exploits, but two of the sisters grew suspicious. They couldn't deal with his strange blue beard and rejected his advances. Undeterred, Bluebeard persuaded the youngest sister to marry him.
>
> She lived with him at his castle in the woods, and one day he had

---

*Excerpt from Heidi Kolb, "Bluebeard ~ A Killer to Reckon With: How to Survive the Soul's Predator," Heidikolb's Blog, September 18, 2010. Used with permission from Heidi M. Kolb, Jungian analyst.

to leave on business. Bluebeard told his wife she could do whatever she wanted while he was away and handed her an enormous bundle of keys. She was free to go into any room she liked, except for one. He showed her the forbidden key, which was the smallest of them all, and then rode off into the woods.

She invited her sisters over and together they explored the castle, opening doors and rifling through cupboards. They found a door in the cellar that fit the tiny key and flung it open without a thought. One brought a candle and held it into the room. *The horror!* Piled in the corner were the skeletons of all Bluebeard's previous wives rotting in the dark, the floor slick with blood.

The sisters screamed and ran away, but the wife just stood there, taking it all in before noticing the key was stained with blood. She tried to wipe it on her dress, but more blood poured from the tiny key. She tried everything she could to stop the flow, but it wouldn't stop. Finally, she hid the key and tried to forget what she had seen.

Bluebeard returned home and asked for his keys back, and immediately noticed one was missing. Enraged, he dragged her to the cellar and opened the terrible door, determined to add to his dead wife collection. But she pleaded with him to allow her time to compose herself and prepare for death. He agreed and gave her fifteen minutes—*more than enough!*

She ran upstairs and called her sisters to look out for her brothers, who were at this very moment racing to her rescue. She knelt and prayed while her sisters watched the horizon. Soon they heard Bluebeard coming up the stairs, roaring for his wife to come to her doom. At that moment, her brothers arrived and ran into the castle. They drew their swords and hacked Bluebeard to pieces and left him for the buzzards, who were most grateful for the feast.*

---

*Excerpt from Jessica Davidson, "Surviving Bluebeard: How to Deal with the Predator," Jessica Davidson: Writer, Storyteller, Fire Stealer (website), January 6, 2015. Used with permission from Jessica Davidson.

Bluebeard is alive and activated in the outer manifest world. In his densest form, a person—usually, but not always, a male—becomes identified with Bluebeard's energy and manifests as a serial killer (yes, they do exist) or a rapist, or as a human trafficker or, as in my case, the predatory spiritual teacher. Many of his victims won't live to tell their story or they remain silent because they are too afraid to speak up. This, in my opinion, is a spiritual death and a travesty. Being silent when the truth needs to be spoken is what the predator relies on for the furtherance of his/her agenda.

Even more prevalent is the sadistic, wife-beating husband. Sadly, in most societies, this kind of abuse is still met by turning a blind eye and saying nothing. We have been conditioned to think that it's "wrong" to interfere with other people's marriages, and that what goes on behind closed doors is none of our business. That is the trap! That kind of thinking is precisely how this depravity continues to take place in our communities. Finally, in the United Kingdom after all these centuries, domestic and emotional abuse in marriages is now classified as a serious crime that comes with a five-year prison sentence.

We want to be wise and not make the mistake of thinking Bluebeard is always a male aggressor. Women are equally capable of allowing this Bluebeard energy to work through them. All forms of excessive and repetitive emotionally abusive behavior is a sign you are being used for dark manipulation. There is a violence that can be inflicted on a (wo)man's (and the perpetrator's) Soul, which draws blood—not from the physical but from the subtle body. This injury can be even more devastating than its physical counterpart. Sadly, it's ignored or played down by society.

The emotionally abusive person is often a pathological narcissist, unwilling/unable to genuinely feel for anyone (including their own feeling self), although they can be sentimental and whiny when it comes to their own needs. Because they are disconnected from a nourishing center in their psyche, they always put themselves and their ego into the center of their lonely universe. Their alienation from the Source forces the pathological narcissist to take more and more drastic measures. They violently seek to pierce through to a reality that will fully support them. That often leaves a trail of blood and corpses, sometimes symbolically, sometimes literally. It is horrifying in both instances.

Going back to our Bluebeard tale, our naïve heroine, who fell for the deadly charmer, survives, and Bluebeard is dismembered and killed. But if a fairy tale is a map, what do we learn about the right kind of attitude to escape Bluebeard? A few things stand out for me. Naïve as the young woman may be, she is not submissive and obedient. It is her disobedience that in fact allows her to survive. In this tale, she must become a warrior for life and then lie to the liar. Like is cured by like. When she opens the door to the torture chamber, she truly sees. She does not escape into fantasies, as so many women in abusive relationships do: "It won't happen to me, he really loves me, he will change," and so on. Nor is she plagued by feelings of paralyzing shame for having been so terribly betrayed (an irrational, but all-too-common response to abuse). When she sees, she knows, and there is no more turning back.

Another question we must ask is this: Why did Bluebeard give her the key to the forbidden room? Was it to test her fidelity to him? Or to see whether she had a mind of her own? Or was it so that she could open the door, giving Bluebeard (a) the excuse to kill her or (b) the realization that she knew her own mind? These are fascinating contemplations to feel into. And if you've already met a Bluebeard, then these are questions you must answer.

Our willingness and strength to face the truth are activating positive masculine energies in us, which manifest in our ability to sever the ties of a Bluebeard's seductive charm. Bluebeard's power is fading. His dismemberment has begun. Our own inner masculinity is gaining muscle, which the fairy tale depicts in the sudden appearance of brothers who put an end to Bluebeard. As an archetypal force Bluebeard will not disappear, but he has no more hold over this woman.

Davidson goes on to "dismember" the story of Bluebeard.

Bluebeard's victim is **the youngest sister** because she's naïve enough to fall for his superficial charm. As a young girl, she represents innocence and the creative potential of life. She could also stand for the Soul itself since this is the object of the predator's murderous intentions.

We can encounter the predator internally as part of our own minds, or externally as part of normal life. He comes in all shapes, but whatever form he takes, the predator is always a light-stealer and consciousness killer. The young and the naïve are prime targets, although he can still get you when you're old if you don't know what to watch for. Girls and women are particularly open to abuse because they're societally and culturally trained to "be nice" and conciliatory. And smile.

Losing touch with our instincts can also make us easy prey. When this happens you're too easily fooled by the surface of things, too willing to overlook the strange blue beard that makes you uneasy. **You collude in your own downfall,** whether through naivety, stupidity, cowardice, laziness, loneliness, greed, lust, wilful rebellion, peer pressure, fantasy, or cultural norms.

Innocence must be outgrown. It's a harsh lesson but a necessary one, and perhaps the Soul engineers the whole thing, as we'll see. . . .

So, through innocence or wilful blindness, you've jumped into bed with the predator, but there's still a part of your psyche that understands what's going on. This is represented in the story by the two older sisters. Even when things are bad, there's usually a part of you that knows where you went wrong and what to do about it. So, the sisters in this tale stand for consciousness or knowledge.

Freedom to Know

Bluebeard tells his wife that she is free to do whatever she wants, except for one thing: she cannot know the truth. The predator always tries to make your life smaller, so he can take your light, or consciousness, for himself. **The key is the way out.** It represents permission to self-knowledge, but here's the thing:

Bluebeard is the one who hands over the key!

If he didn't want her to open the door, why give her the key?

Perhaps it's a test of loyalty, perhaps he's setting her up to fail. But it's more likely that he knows she'll open the door. He secretly wants her to open the door. After all, if she doesn't open it, he can't kill her and take her light/soul.

This is a clue that you can't awaken to full self-knowledge without a confrontation with the predator. **Not only do you collude in your own abduction by the darkness, but the darkness contains the key to your awakening.** The predator doesn't want you to be conscious or know who you truly are. He doesn't want you to awaken, but he gives you the key anyway.

If you obey the predator and refuse to use the key, you choose death. But using the key opens you to the secrets of the psyche— all the dead bodies. Perhaps it would be better not to see those terrible things, to stay asleep and not know the truth. If self-knowledge means death and destruction, then unconsciousness seems preferable. But this is an important initiation—a spiritual rite of passage— to gain sovereignty over your own mind and soul. To refuse it, is to refuse to live.

The **door** represents a psychic barrier that stands between you and self-knowledge. Every time you refuse to think for yourself, you keep that door firmly closed and collude with the predator. The destruction of the room represents all the things you've killed in your attempt to "be nice": hopes, dreams, desires, intuitions, potentials.

The **blood on the key** represents your creative juices, your life force leaking away through lack of use, denial or self-destructiveness. The blood pours over the **dress** which represents the persona. This means you can't hide what you've learned—the truth is out. Now you know the predator is out to get you and you've got a fight on your hands.

The predator wants to kill the creative feminine side of the psyche, the part from which all new life arises. This part of the soul is buried deep. It knows the way forward, knows what you need to grow and live a full life. This is where your best insights and potentials come from, but to reach them you must go into the darkness. But that means you also have to deal with the destruction you find there. In other words, **you must accept the darkness and not turn away from it.** You must be willing to face it. That doesn't mean letting the predator have his wicked way with you. It means getting smart.

The **bones** of the dead wives represent the soul—the hardest part of the psyche to destroy. Their flesh may have rotted away, but the bones are still there. Like we see on the Death tarot card, the destruction is a blessing in disguise and rebirth is on its way. This means the situation isn't hopeless—there's life in these old bones yet! The soul is reborn through consciousness, by becoming awake to the truth and breaking the habit of ignorance.

Poison Becomes Medicine

The wife pleads for **time to prepare** for death and the predator, strangely, agrees. This is an important point in the story, even if it doesn't quite make sense. She's buying time to call for help, and you can do that too when confronted by the predator. He tends to pop up whenever you move forward or gain consciousness when things are going well or you're feeling positive. The predator rises up and tries to stop you by killing off the new awareness. He throws cold water over your hopes, like an evil bucket challenge, but you can learn to step out of the way.

The wife calls to her **brothers** who ride to the rescue. The brothers represent the part of the psyche that's ready to fight and kill the predator. It's a fierce self-protective energy that acts in the face of anything that would destroy you (doesn't have to be masculine, has nothing to do with gender).

Bluebeard is **dismembered and eaten** by the birds. This shamanic image hints at a deeper meaning—he's not just killed and forgotten. Finally, the part of the psyche that doesn't want to die (which is the real reason he's a failed magician and going about stealing light) is transformed. He isn't annihilated, but absorbed back into the cycle of life. The **carrion birds** are soul-carriers and sin-eaters who carry the immortal soul to the Otherworld so it can be reborn. In terms of the individual psyche, the predator is recycled—his energy is redirected and transformed into something useful.

In practical terms what this means is that you refuse to agree with the predator when he puts you down. Don't allow yourself to be side-tracked or undermined or devalued. Refuse to be silenced or blinded to the truth. Sidestep the bucket of cold water.

You fight the predator with more consciousness, more awareness, and use his energy for something positive and life-enhancing. So you could take his rage and use it to burn through all the things you no longer need, or pour it into your creative work. Or take his trickiness and cunning and use it to be more discerning.

As with vaccinations where a tiny bit of the poison is used to inoculate you and trigger an immune response which heals the body, **you take the poison of the predator and transmute it into medicine.** To free yourself from the power of the predator all you need to do is see it for what it is. In other words, look at how you collude with your own unconsciousness and create your shadow. Face your fears, think for yourself, and refuse to give away your power.

All easier said than done, but you already have the ultimate weapon at your disposal: your true nature. Your deep soul wisdom or Self knows how to live. When you're in a potentially dangerous situation, she's the one who whispers in your ear, *"Stop being so nice,"* *"Stop smiling,"* and *"Can't you see he's got a knife?"*

She's also the birds that sing when you need cheering up, the sun that comes out at just the right moment, and on the day you decided to give up for good, she's the dog that appears on your path and makes you laugh and change your mind.*

---

*Excerpt from Jessica Davidson, "Surviving Bluebeard: How to Deal with the Predator," Jessica Davidson: Writer, Storyteller, Fire Stealer (website), January 6, 2015. Used with permission from Jessica Davidson.

ARCHONS

The Forces of Anti-Awakening

The Archons are known as the rulers, servants, or influential powers of the Dark Agenda. According to the Gnostic Gospel of Philip, the Archons' main objective is to keep humans ignorant of their Divine origins beyond the physical universe. They are the seven great influences that make up the seven deadly sins whose transgressions are fatal to our spiritual progress.

Let me say that again: whose transgressions are fatal to our spiritual progress.

Many in the New Age will say that these astral creatures do not exist, that they are a figment of our imaginations. This, my beloved friends, is not true. There are plenty of things that exist inside and outside of us, and these agents of chaos are real and are close at any given moment. They hold the world of control in place by invoking thoughts that create emotions that result in actions. If we are not aware, we become their puppets, their playthings motivated by fear and tension.

The Archons answer only to their creator, something far more destructive than we would ever want to know. It's not worth going there—it's too big, too ancient, and too everywhere—but what we can do is relinquish the Archonic ability to hook into our minds and orchestrate our lives in its favor.

When we become super aware, we can sense them coming in. I personally can smell them with my inner nose. There is an uneasy aroma of artificial tendencies; a field of anti-love, anti-life, and cruel intention. Like the "déjà vu" scene in *The Matrix,* we notice a glitch in our awareness. A hunch that something is not right, and lo and behold they will start "suggesting" unnatural things to you inside your head.

Now, before you go off exclaiming paranoid tendencies, take a breath and understand that humanity has been living alongside these things since the beginning of time. Every great tradition has performed rituals and ceremonies to protect themselves from these influences. At every sunrise and sundown the Gnostics, Essenes, and Cathars (to name a few) would pray for clear sight, protection, and humility. But for some reason, we have stopped doing that. I think we believe that these things don't exist anymore, or that we have outgrown them.

I'm not sure that's such a good thing to be thinking . . .

It is said that the Archons do not carry within them the spark of the Divine, that they have been created out of a being who is false, without love, and motivated by separation. It is at this point the New Agers jump in to say that nothing like this can exist. That is not true. And this is how the game continues on.

The Archon Agenda

What do the Archons want? To maintain the world of control. To keep us preoccupied with fear, separation, and chaos, resulting in us eating more, buying more, drinking more, smoking more, working harder, taking drugs (pharmaceutical and recreational), creating war, buying weaponry, being hostile, killing off people, killing off animals, killing off land—in other words, manipulating us to be like them, so that we maintain the life they're accustomed to!

This is not to pass the buck so to speak but to inform and bring awareness of our own sovereignty. It's so vital for us be aware of our breath and to check in with ourselves regularly when we make choices by asking ourselves: "Am I fully behind what I'm saying?" "Is this me speaking?" "Is this my choice?"

When you notice that an Archonic influence might be whispering in your ear, declare from the center of your heart: "I am a sovereign being, and you have no hold on me. I am not part of your world, and you have no power over me."

Breathe steadily and deeply. Choose love. Choose life. Choose goodness.

And it will pass.

Maybe we have come across a person being taken over by an Archon. The level of rage, insanity, destruction, and mayhem is inhuman. Personally, I see this in some of our leaders. The level of war that can come through this kind of person does not reflect the emotional capacity that a human being is wired for. It surpasses everything we have ever seen. And so, if we have met one, we will know it.

Archons cannot be saved. Archons cannot be healed. Archons are not to be messed with. I respectfully acknowledge their presence in either myself or others and pray for their passing.

Rather than go to war with these beings, my path is to choose my sovereignty and to align myself with courage and humility to come to prayer and goodness. This is not something I take lightly. It is a real and vulnerable moment. A real choice between life and death.

Back in the day, we would have called them evil spirits. But what we must realize is that as we have grown, they have grown, and I sense their mission now is to sabotage and halt our progression toward awakening. There is so much at stake. Humans are a powerful workforce, generating much energy, money, creativity, art, innovation, and emotional currency. If we are able to take back our power and guide it toward a destination of our choosing, which we can and must do, then a whole new level of existence will come into view. If, however, we stay as fodder for the Archons, then I suspect we and they, along with their creator, will eventually annihilate ourselves—because that is all that can happen.

Perhaps by witnessing our beingness of sovereignty, our choosing of goodness by taking back our power of choice and being fully and radiantly in our hearts, they too will one day opt to serve something else. I don't know. But I will give them the benefit of the doubt, if there is such a thing.

I often wonder whether our current spiritual fascination and pastime is part of the Dark Agenda. In my observation, it attempts to psychically cripple us in so many dangerous ways. False spirituality, narcissistic teachers, toxic practices, and the "specialness" of being in an inner circle have made up the hubris that we have called the Spiritual Path. This is not spirituality; this is a trap, and a deadly one. This kind of environment feeds the spiritual ego, and this is a place where many of us have ended up or will soon. It takes quantum amounts of humility and softening to step out of this place. Sometimes the only way is a very severe collapse and falling apart of both the structure of the community and the coming to terms with the illusion in our own self.

SPIRITUAL MYTHS
CREATED BY THE DARK AGENDA

Here is the great manifesto of false spirituality. Have a read through these recognizable statements, and tread carefully when you hear someone saying these are the absolute truth.

There is nothing outside of us. Untrue, there is plenty outside of us interfering, influencing, coercing, and tampering with our perception and reactions. There is a whole host of influences with us at any given moment.

We are all one. Maybe this is true in the long run. But to discover whether that is true in the now, we must develop our eyes to clearly see the agendas and distortions being placed over us. And then decide whether we want to be one with that or not.

Nothing outside of you has any real power. Oh yes, it does, but unless we truly know "there is no spoon," as the young boy states calmly to Neo in *The Matrix,* we will be bombarded with "agents" that interfere and usurp our power, and we won't even know it—until we do.

It's all love. Maybe. But until we have completed this journey and have fully restored our wisdom, there are many steps and stages along the path that are anti-loving, anti-awakening, and agents of false truth and false humility. I personally do not believe that these "qualities" have anything to do with any form of love I have ever come across.

There is no truth to be found "out there." I disagree. I believe the biggest threat to the Dark Agenda is people gathering and sharing information and healing and awakening modalities and exchanging natural and sustaining ideas. I believe that truth can be shared among people through interaction and communication.

All negative observations are projections. Perhaps, but perhaps not. If we believe and live like that, we shall be rendered an ineffective, passive, and impotent fence-sitter in a time when we must be extremely active. Perhaps what we think of as projection is, in fact, genuine and accurate intuition. To turn our back on that innate gift, as the New Age suggests, is to relinquish our deeper knowing and psychic navigational skills.

To fully heal you should leave your partner. If our partner is not abusing us in any way, perhaps the greater truth would be, *To fully heal stay with our partner.*

You need to leave your friends and family behind. Red flag warning! We are most likely being coerced into an isolating situation where we are going to slowly be broken down. There may be a time where we would be wise to step back from friends and family, especially if we have become enmeshed. But this is done in the name of empowerment, a place where you can love and acknowledge them more, not less.

I can heal you if you have sex with me. This is the one that has hoodwinked so many. And this is the most dangerous one, because now we are adding more trauma and more wounding to a person who is already in a weakened and fragile state. No matter how attractive, how magnetic, or how powerful the teacher or any member of the facilitation team, the exchange of sex for healing is not found to be in the hands of men—yet. The kind of sex I am referring to here has a dark agenda and intention and originates from a negative situation. The act of sex as a healing modality is a true offering and can indeed lead to profound wellness and healing in the entire being. But the one who cleanly gifts such a thing is a very rare and precious find.

Within our inner and outer reality there's a whole host of forces and influences being orchestrated that can at times be clearly seen, but are mostly felt. They are the agents of the Dark Agenda whose job it is to keep us inactive and fearful by encouraging us to give our power away to the agents that come in via our thought forms, mood swings, movies, music, digital technology, and most of all, social media. The Fierce Feminine Rising is the biggest threat to the Dark Agenda because Her natural response is to gather together, to communicate, to share, to cross-pollinate, to encourage, to heighten, and to inform the direction of our genuine spiritual awakening.

If the people gather and regain their inner knowing, the Dark Agenda will crumble. Why? Because we will "see" the wool before it gets pulled over our eyes. We will "hear" the motive and agenda before the words get spoken. And we will "feel" the presence of a dark atmosphere and not be afraid of it anymore. Instead, we will challenge its assumed authority and pull the plug on its limited hold over us. However, this will never happen if we do not come together and share our knowledge openly and without assuming hierarchy. And no good can come if only the world of humans is being considered.

QUESTIONS WE MUST ASK

If we are to survive the initiation of meeting the Archons and Bluebeards of this world, then we must ask the kinds of questions that cause the secret doors of the psyche to open. Take out a pen and paper now and answer the following questions:

- Have you met an Archon/Bluebeard?
- At what point did you start to collude with your own downfall? At what point did you say, "Maybe his beard isn't really that blue?" or "Surely, we won't go that far?" What was in it for you personally—riches, status, sex?
- Did you secretly know what was going on and in some ways invoke it? Was there a dream where you chose the dark man? Did you know at some stage of life you would have to face this

ordeal? If yes, why were you made aware of this? And what was that awareness doing, as you lived it?

Bluebeard Questions

- Did you realize you were given a key?
- Do you feel he wanted to test your fidelity or have a reason to kill you and take your Light?
- Where do you think that door is, and what might lie behind it?
- When did you notice that the key was bleeding and falling on your dress?
- Could you hear the voices of your two older sisters? What were they telling you?
- What did you do while you had your fifteen minutes to pray?
- When the poison turns into medicine, what will it be used for?
- Who or what were the older brothers?

Archon Questions

- Why have you been made aware of Archonic influence?
- What are they afraid you will discover?
- How can you make regular contact with that part of you?
- Are you able to identify the kinds of scenarios they show up in?
- What emotions do they conjure inside of you?
- What fortifying attitude could you take to halt their influence over you?
- What ways can you identify them?
- What does the true Self say to you, the one that is free from Archonic interference?

Death of the Oceans

Our oceans are in an unnatural state. There is nothing bleaker and more apocalyptic when we realize that 29 percent of the seafood species we consume have already been wiped out. We have been warned and warned again that unless we make immediate changes, by the time we reach 2048, if we reach 2048 that is, there may be no more fish in any of our seas or oceans.[*] Every year, approximately 17–22 percent of seafood brought out of the ocean is then thrown back in—usually dead or dying.[†] But still, we continue overfishing and acidifying the ocean, imagining—or rather being in denial—that our actions are just and warranted.

The World Wildlife Fund notes,

---

[*]John Roach, "Seafood May Be Gone by 2048, Study Says," National Geographic (website), November 2, 2006.

[†]Amanda Keledijan, Gib Brogan, Beth Lowell, et al. "Wasted Catch: Unsolved Problems in U.S. Fisheries," Oceana: Protecting the World's Oceans (website), March 2014.

Some 4 million fishing vessels of all sizes now ply the oceans, many with increasing capacity and efficiencies to catch more fish. As pressure from fishing grows, the likelihood of damage to the structure and function of the ocean ecosystem increases. Inadequate government capacity and cooperation to manage, regulate, and control fisheries and fisheries trade, especially in developing nations and on the high seas, are key factors contributing to the current problems in oceanic fisheries.*

You may be asking why so many fish are being caught, and why the sudden increase? It's simple—human overpopulation. And this doesn't only mean more humans wanting to eat more fish. One-third of the fish caught is used for animal feed.† Pigs are eating more fish than sharks, which begs the question—what kind of world are we living in? There is nothing sustainable that we know of in our oceans, because we have depleted everything that we are aware of. Eventually, our oceans will fall silent as every whale and dolphin conversation becomes drowned out by the increasingly noisy sound of the death machine up above.

Operation Apex Harmony notes that over 90 percent of the world's sharks have been killed through fishing, shark finning, and shark mitigation strategies and that 70 to 100 million sharks continue to die each year. This means over 10,000 sharks die every hour and, they go on to note, "Few know, often blinded by misguided fears, of the shark's current struggles and the impact this could have on human life. Sharks are quickly headed for extinction."‡ Even though we have been taught to think about the cycle of life as a food chain, the truth is that most marine ecosystems are more like a food web, with complex and yet unknown interconnections among the different animals. So when we take one or several players out of this interdependent food web, the consequences are uncertain.

---

*World Wildlife Fund, "Overfishing," WWF website.
†Deborah Zabarenko, "One-Third of World Fish Catch Used for Animal Feed," Reuters (website), October 29, 2008.
‡"Why Are Sharks Important?" Operation Apex Harmony, Sea Shepherd (website).

It's not merely overfishing that's the problem; the acidification of the ocean is an equal threat. Smithsonian's Ocean Portal Team notes,

> Ocean acidification is sometimes called "climate change's equally evil twin," and for good reason: it's a significant and harmful consequence of excess carbon dioxide in the atmosphere that we don't see or feel because its effects are happening underwater. At least one-quarter of the carbon dioxide (CO_2) released by burning coal, oil and gas doesn't stay in the air, but instead dissolves into the ocean. Since the beginning of the industrial era, the ocean has absorbed some 525 billion tons of CO_2 from the atmosphere, presently around 22 million tons per day.[*]

Without a functioning ocean ecosystem we don't have a functioning atmosphere and without a functioning atmosphere, we will literally be dead. Even if we stopped our carbon emissions now, it will be many centuries before the oceans return to their full health. Make no mistake: we rely on our oceans more than we realize. Not only are they an incredible carbon sink, but they also provide the world with half of all its oxygen. Many of us already realize that it's too late for climate change and pollution to be stamped out. All that is left then, as seen from our current vantage point, is the transformation of our oceans from cornucopias of life to graveyards that we can only describe in elegiac terms. World War II will be a footnote compared to what we're doing right now to cause the loss of biodiversity.

Pause here for reflection. Take the time that is needed to truly be with these insights and understandings. Just breathe and be with them. Let's bear witness to the sobriety of the situation and feel one another as we rise together to receive more of Her transmission.

Let's move on without answers.

We must learn to trust the process, remembering that *this is an initiation*.

---

[*]The Ocean Portal Team, "Ocean Acidification," reviewed by Jennifer Bennett (NOAA), Smithsonian Ocean (website), April 2018.

Part Two
· · · · · · · · · · ·

Taking Back
Our Power

FOUR
The Dark Night of the Soul
Healing Our Sacred Wounds

THE PHRASE "DARK NIGHT OF THE SOUL" describes a prolonged period of emotional and spiritual desolation in which there is seemingly no consolation. It can feel like a collapse of the perceived meaning in our lives. It hurts, and it's meant to. Usually, at first, there is a sense of loss or betrayal, but after time, should we surrender to the process, the suffering becomes transformed into a spiritual gift of pure gold.

A true dark night of the soul leaves a lasting impact on us—it changes us completely. When we exit a dark night, we discover that something has been taken away from us and lifted from our shoulders.

I believe I have experienced two dark nights. The first one was only a taste, a baby version of what was to come. Whereas the last dark night felt like I had been snatched by a strong-willed and relentless crocodile who was determined to take me down into the cold, black water with no hope of escape.

I choked, I spluttered, I gasped for air. But there wasn't any. There was only pain, only suffering and the sense of an ever-growing isolation. I felt abandoned by God, abandoned by life, and abandoned by myself. There was nothing I could do but writhe in agony and pray, begging and crying out for relief. But relief does not come—for some time anyway. That is what makes a dark night a dark night. It is meant to last for a long time so the Soul can descend down and down and down into the dark matter of unconscious debris, trauma, and wounding.

Finally, one morning I noticed a tiny little shaft of Light on the inside and I knew it was me, the true me. It was the version of me I recognized from childhood. It was gentle, pure, and kind. This presence nourished me and helped me rebuild my confidence. And this little Light grew and grew and grew until it became a golden heart of pure passion and power. And now I know for sure—God does not abandon us, S/He only looks away, so we're able to see beyond Her/Him.

Out of suffering have emerged the strongest souls; the most massive characters are seared with scars.

KHALIL GIBRAN

A dark night is not a period of depression or fatigue. It is an alive-and-kicking spiritual-death process. It could emerge because of a terminal diagnosis, old age, a near-death experience, a physical accident, the loss of a loved one, a romantic breakup, the destruction of your home or homeland, suicidal depression, or the complete loss of your religious faith. The dark night is a herald or an omen of change. It lets us know that we can't continue living the way we have been living. There is no growth and no awakening to life without first seeing and acknowledging our existing disappointment.

Acknowledging our disappointment means becoming aware of the deeply held sense of "incompletion" that we all carry. It means becoming aware that something is desperately missing from our lives. Those that have experienced or are currently experiencing a dark night of the soul will know that something very fundamental at a core level is out of focus or completely lacking in their lives. Those going through a dark night will sense that so much more is possible in their lives, even though they don't exactly know what that "so much more" is.

It is this heartbreak that shatters the masks and pretense and sends us straight into Spirit as we plunge into an existential crisis. And this is good. Because now we are in the terrain of genuine spiritual transformation.

Below are seven signs that together signify we may be going through a dark night of the soul:

1. Feeling a deep sense of sadness, which often verges on despair (this sadness is often triggered by the state of our life, humanity, and/or the world as a whole)
2. Feeling an acute sense of unworthiness
3. Feeling lost or "condemned" to a life of suffering or emptiness
4. A painful feeling of powerlessness and hopelessness
5. Weakening of will and self-control, making it difficult to take any actions
6. Lacking interest and finding no joy in things that once were exciting
7. Craving the loss of something intangible; a longing for a distant place or to "return home" again

Both women and men have access to a voice that is prophetic, outraged, splendorous, and uncomfortably truthful. We are all challenged by our different temperaments in ways to align ourselves with this voice. But we all must let that voice—that voice of truth, impetuous and scalding, vibrant truth—rise in us because that's Her voice. And that's the voice that will help us protect life, before it's destroyed. This is about burning alive in the fire of the Fierce Feminine and speaking with the voice of her pure lucid, lacerating, laser-clear flame of truth. We must feel into the belly of a lioness and dare to roar to protect our lion children.

There are three ways that spiritual awakenings can occur: the first is at the hands of wise teachers, the second is through the pursuit of soulfully mature people, and the third is spontaneously from life experience.

Once we figure out we're going through a dark night of the soul, what then?

The dark night of the soul is an important and valuable spiritual gift. It may not be seen or felt that way in the moment, but in hindsight, we will look back and see it was exactly that. If we are able, the wisest first step is to create a space where we will not be disturbed. We need to be able to give ourselves the permission, the time, and the space to be able to surrender to the dark night process. We never know how long it's going to take, so perhaps start off with a three-month sabbatical. Looking back, I can see that the dark night came in waves and levels of intensity. Learn to navigate the various stages and then act accordingly.

If we can surrender to the dark night, the journey may become more easeful, and move more quickly through us, than if we resist. So really, it's best to go with the process, rather than against it.

An ideal situation would be a log cabin in the woods or a quiet house-sit for a friend, or maybe a reclusive ashram setting or vipassana retreat. One thing I advise: do not delay! Take your essential items only. Leave behind your laptop, your cell phone, your work, your responsibilities, your job, and your social life. Only bring the things that can serve your surrender. If it is impossible for you to do this, what is most important is the ability to be alone. You are being called in, and it's essential that you go there. So even if it's just one weekend or one evening that you have to spare, dedicate it to simple being-ness. Lay down and feel your feelings. Turn in, breathe deeply, be with yourself.

When I went through the dark night—for me, the coming away from an abusive and powerful cult and at the same time initiating a painful divorce—I was cat- and house-sitting for a friend. My only daily activity was a long walk to the gym, where I would do an hour-long strenuous aerobics class. During that class, I would cry so deeply, but no one noticed as my face was drenched in sweat. I am certain this bodily exertion gave me a powerful channel to release my grief and prevent it from getting stuck. After the gym, I would walk home through a beautiful park and sit under a specific cherry blossom tree. I struck up a relationship with that tree; it became my beacon of hope and only friend during that time. Every day I noticed the new blossoms that had appeared and prayed that this tree could one day be a reflection of me. It was these kinds of vulnerable, innocent exchanges with life that brought so much healing. Life seemed to slow, and it was the simple things that brought in grace.

I couldn't interact with others during that time because I would always start crying. The grief was so deep and unruly that I felt uncomfortable revealing it to others. It was far easier to be my messy, hurt, broken self under that cherry tree. For the rest of the day, I would either return to bed or journal in my diary. This provided an essential outlet for words and feelings to be expressed and for partial wisdom to be revealed. Looking back, I can see how this insular process brought me back to myself. I was retrieving parts of me that had been frozen in anguish and fear. During this five-month phase, I lost so much weight and vitality. Yet deep inside I knew I was doing okay. I felt as if the extra weight carried buried emotions, and the more I cried, the more the weight slid from my bones.

Once I had gone through that initial stripping-away process I felt I needed to gift myself with a beautiful experience to say thank you for all the deep work I had been doing. I also wanted to nourish myself and be warmed by the sun. I felt I was entering a new phase of the journey, which I called the Return to Life. So I booked a flight to Maui, where I planned to stay in a yurt for one month. This area was once again remote but had a sprinkling of a community close by. Maui was incredible! The nature was so vibrant and alive—just the right place for phase 2. The roundedness of the yurt was such a godsend. It enabled me to feel safe and held, while the closeness of the earth provided that deep feeling of support. I thrived in this environment, my thin greying appearance truly blossomed into that cherry tree. Slowly, slowly, slowly I ventured to the local juice bar and started to make friends. It felt strange and awkward to speak to others. But on Maui, it was so much easier, as everyone was so open and natural. It wasn't long before I took a vast and unknown step—I agreed to go to a gathering! And it was at this *bhajan* concert where I met a beloved brother who was able to gently interact with me in ways that I thought were impossible to ever experience again.

After my time in Maui, it was back to the healing process to begin phase 3—deeper release. I accepted an invitation to live with a more mature friend in her huge country house in Belgium. I had my own quarter of the house, so I knew I would be left alone, and also nature was right on the doorstep. During this time, I headed straight into the uncomfortable psychic material that needed to be gone through. This was the introspection phase, where I examined the how, the why, and the what. I felt I needed to understand how I attracted this ordeal into my life, and what I learned from it. It was like an inner organization process, where I discarded some things and enshrined others.

All in all, the most precious elements of the dark night are surrender, solitude, gentleness, prayer, and reestablishing a healing relationship with one's Self. And if there's the inclination to do so, eat a diet of fresh and simple foods, drink plenty of water, rest and sleep as much as possible throughout the day. Spend as much time as possible in bed as well. Get out in nature but don't force anything. Connecting with nature and performing some simple rituals is highly recommended. The mind is going to be obliterated so there's no point in thinking or planning or strategizing or trying to even understand what's happening—it's beyond the mind's grasp. Openly inform family and friends of what is happening; there's nothing to be ashamed of. Take this time without indulging any feelings of guilt. True-and-trusted friends and family will hold the space for your eventual return.

Wise Words for the Dark Night*

- Keep practicing: Don't give up spiritual practice, even if it seems pointless or scary.
- Have faith: Remember that we are not in control of this process. Be guided by something greater, without trying to control it.
- Stay open: Remain open to whatever comes up, good or bad. Say yes to it all. Don't resist.

*Adapted from Jessica Davidson, "How to Survive the Dark Night of the Soul," Jessica Davidson: Writer, Storyteller, Fire Stealer (website). June 23, 2014. Used with permission from Jessica Davidson.

- Rest: Allow for sleep—at all times of day/night.
- Connect with nature: Find the cherry blossom tree. Walk, breathe, talk, pray, whisper, return to nature.
- Maintain perspective: Don't go too far with extreme practices to heal "faster."
- Humor: Maintain a sense of humor; it's vital to surviving the worst of the dark night.
- Embrace the darkness: Learn to trust the dark. Dispel the darkness by bringing more consciousness to it. See darkness as a reflective space to let go into.
- Exercise: It's incredibly grounding to exercise regularly. Go for walks, do yoga, breathe consciously, dance your dance of sorrow— anything that provides movement and focuses on the body. Otherwise, it's easy to get lost in the head.
- Practice self-inquiry: Break down the components of the experience by deconstructing thoughts and feelings during meditation practice. Remember to ask the right questions: Who is thinking? Who is scared? Who is dying? Who is going stark raving bonkers?! (There's that humor again!)
- Find a teacher: Find someone to guide you through the process but be sure they have been through it themselves. If you can't find someone, then read spiritual literature, particularly Ramana Maharshi, Gangaji, St. John of the Cross, or Teresa of Avila.
- Bless yourself: Nourish yourself. Pray to yourself. Speak kindly to yourself, inside and outside. Wish yourself well.

Eventually, once the dark night has lifted, we will realize that we have been resurrected from the ashes of our past. This gruelling process has turned us into an even more loving human being who is aware and together. There's a sense of being spiritually detoxed and completely connected to all with such a genuine and grateful attitude. All regret, shame, and frustration has thinned and disappeared. There is a sense of having turned a corner, and all that is before us is now a clean and clear blank page. This is a glorious moment, a real encounter of grace.

The most important thing to remember is this: the dark night is a deep and essential healing process. Pain and illusions are being removed from us; we must let them go.

GLOBAL DARK NIGHT OF THE SOUL

I believe we are currently in a global dark night of the soul. I expect by the time you read this, the distinction between the personal and the global dark night won't mean anything anymore. I think, for the feminine, there is no separation between personal and global. We simply take the pain of the broken world into the cells of our body, where we hold and listen to the grief cries from those who are seen and unseen. This is how it is, but I wonder what would happen if we got conscious about this?

I think back to the 2018 movie *Mary Magdalene* where we get to see Mary truly standing as the embodiment of the first witness of the resurrection. She is the one who gets to see and converse with the risen Christ. In the biblical texts, we are led to believe this was a chance meeting with a grieving and desperate Mary who was sobbing outside Yeshua's tomb.

But that is not the story that lives in my heart. Instead, I believe that rather than asking Mary to be his witness, Yeshua stated that she would be. That it would be Mary that not only observed the transfiguration but absorbed it. This form of witnessing was a soaking up of a transmission radiated through and by the passion of a human becoming Divine, Yeshua becoming Christ.

And this is precisely what I sense the role of the feminine could be in the global dark night of the soul. Should we become not only conscious but willing to soak up the despair of the world as an active witness, could it be that this act becomes the transforming catalyst that enables a global transfiguration?

Perhaps I could go a step further and say that Yeshua's transfiguration was for Mary, so she could witness the absolute Truth of who she was and finally accept that it was she who was the Messiah—his promised deliverer. Her witnessing birthed Christ. Could our witnessing also birth something we are currently unaware of?

I feel it is so.

I believe it is this very quality of Mary Magdalene that touches so many women. For she was with him until the very end, enduring, witnessing, and feeling her way through the process. I see this as a reverse birth. A woman ready, willing, and able to birth her beloved into Divinity with all the pain, suffering, ecstasy, and glory that goes with giving birth in physical form.

Many women recognize what she did. They may not be able to verbalize it or comprehend it fully, but they know. Most likely they long to do the same, to meet their beloved and to birth them into Divinity. And I believe that is precisely what Mary would have wanted us to do. However, it may not be a man this time around, but rather the world. Maybe this is one of Mary Magdalene's messages.

Why would we do such a thing?

Because we can. We are currently the fifth root race. There have been four earlier attempts at human life on this planet. And four times humanity has died out. So we know that human extinction is possible. My question is this: Were the previous races conscious of what was happening, or were they only aware of the catastrophe and chaos? I wonder, what would or what could happen if we chose to go through this consciously?

So instead of turning away when we see pictures of barbaric acts of cruelty and neglect toward animals or read that a million tons of radioactive water are still in storage after the nuclear disaster in Fukushima or turn yet another page or scroll down, inwardly groaning when we realize Google plans to project their logo onto the surface of the moon or feel sick to our stomach when we see live footage of people on dairy farms kicking the cows and calling them cunts . . . let's stop, witness, breathe, and absorb the truth of what's happening all around us every day. Let us be gracious enough to notice the pain and ignorance of our dying race and our insane and heinous crimes against the world. Let us partake in this last act while great hope burns in our heart for a new future with our merciful prayer that we are included.

SACRED WOUNDS

Healing Our Soul's Sorrow

A sacred wound is caused by a spiritual trauma or existing crisis that often involves some form of loss and betrayal—the same circumstances that trigger the dark night. A sacred wound is always associated with a form of service to others of a spiritual nature. There's a theme that unites them all: spiritual betrayal of the highest order and the sense that things have been left undone, broken, or unattended. When we look at the nature of betrayal, there is always a sense of broken trust. And when the betrayal is of epic proportions, imagine how searing that broken trust must feel.

However, there's some good news with regard to these wounds, and that is: the deeper the trust, the deeper the betrayal; the deeper the wound, the greater the blessing! That, my beloved friend, is the sacred wound, and I suspect not everyone has one. But if you do, you'll know it! These are my people—the spiritually wounded and the Soul warriors. The tattered, ragged, weary, but still standing Bravehearts of the world. The scar tissue of a sacred wound doesn't go away with some ho'oponopono, or prayers for forgiveness. It takes grounded, mystical work to get into the holy vault within the Soul where the bloodied dagger lies. The way forward will be different for everyone, but I believe at the edge of every sacred wound there is some place of pure meeting, where the hurt is appeased by grace in whatever form it takes. What we can do is swim through the murky waters of darkness and into the depths of suffering, face the pain, and come out into a new place—one that we could have never found without pain, one that looks like grace.

If you meet someone with a sacred wound, be gentle with them. If you carry one, be gentle with yourself.

Sorrow prepares you for joy. It violently sweeps everything out of your house, so that new joy can find space to enter. It shakes the yellow leaves from the bough of your heart, so that fresh, green leaves can grow in their place. It pulls up the rotten roots, so that new roots hidden beneath have room to grow. Whatever sorrow shakes from your heart, far better things will take their place.

RUMI

I believe if we are blessed, we shall get to occasionally glimpse and feel the existential sorrow threaded throughout the Soul. It seems there is a pasture that we often find ourselves in, where we stumble across the rabbit hole that takes us down deep into the beautiful travesties of our lives. We get to witness fleeting phantoms of our own Self, sometimes in the guise of an exiled priestess, tortured martyr, misunderstood ET, fallen angel, or excommunicated truth-teller.

I often wonder why these streams of consciousness wander through our realm, and why they seem to be more widespread than ever before. For a start, I don't believe they are necessarily the reflections of our past lives, but rather the archetypes that walk within us quietly tugging at us for release, since they too are in this dark night and waiting for transformation. I am quite certain this great global dark night that we are now experiencing will draw absolutely everything into its swirling spirals of rebirth. Everything that we have ever known consciously and unconsciously will be affected, and that includes the archetypes. These impersonal patterns of influence that are both ancient and universal are so outdated, their stories so heavy and worn. They have been leaning into our personality, drives, feelings, beliefs, motivations, and actions forever. However, these archetypes are not passive entities floating around in our psyche like ghosts. They are ancient guardians of wisdom, who must be honored as they leave our domain.

SACRED WOUNDS AND
THEIR GIFTS

The sacred wounds and their gifts started to come to me during Easter of 2018. I believe that I carried a sacred wound, and finally, after many years, it had been healed. I had held within me the wound of the High Priestess. This particular wound contains a tremendous guilt and the incessant drive to make everything spiritually "right" this time. A sacred wound is caused by a spiritual trauma that often involves some form of betrayal. And with a betrayal comes broken trust. The deeper the trust, the deeper the betrayal—and the deeper the wound. However, the deeper the wound, the greater the blessing. In order to heal, we have to feel. These wounds beckon us to the very fabric of that spiritual trespass, a place we could easily spend our whole life avoiding.

I have a feeling many things are now coming into view. I often consider whether our sacred wounds may be coming from a time when we cross-pollinated with another race in our ancient and recorded past. Our sacred wounds do appear god(dess)-like. They seem like epic portrayals of a time gone wrong, and perhaps now they return, to forewarn to not do the same thing again. I cannot help but feel there are many beings who support our great rebirth, and many that do not. The ultimate truth being that they are all one and the same.

The Fallen Angel Wound

The wound of the Fallen Angel is the inability to trust or surrender to God. And that is extremely tiring, especially if we know it is inevitable that one day we will. The Fallen Angel appears brilliant, charismatic, and confident—but underneath all that charm and sophistication is a lonely, cold, abandoned child. The Fallen Angel is unable to truly love a human as an intimate. Fallen Angels will feel "different" and that is what keeps them apart. The Fallen Angel thrives on being the rebel and it is precisely this quality these angels must be willing to release. When this wound is healed these angels will feel forgiven through and through. Countless waves of guilt, shame, and regret will be cleansed from them.

The High Priest/Priestess Wound

The wound of the High Priest/Priestess is the guilt that something went horribly wrong in a spiritual way in the past. There is an onus, a great weight of responsibility that bears down upon these people reminding them of how they did/could let others down by their misdeeds. Guilt and shame lie within their body, cornering them off from true spiritual acclaim and accolade. There could also be a staunch denial that must first be embraced and owned. When this wound is healed, this priest/priestess's true ministry will flourish. They will receive unthought-of codes, contributions for the community, and new ceremonial ways of bringing all into direct contact with the Divine.

The Prophet/Prophetess Wound

The wound of the Prophet/Prophetess is to fear being silenced, or that one's words will bring about a deadly outcome. There is a constant hesitation, a fear of speaking up and speaking out, a fear of being hunted for their gifts, or that they could be coerced or misused in some way as they enter the altered state of transmission. There is a sense of "Shall I, shan't I?" when it comes to speaking up. This form of doubt must be lifted from these beloved prophets/prophetesses, for now is the time of the great revelation. When this wound is healed they will not fear the power of their words. They will be one with their word, its voice, and its authority.

The Sacred Prostitute Wound

The wound of the Sacred Prostitute is to be always in service and never in love. The Sacred Prostitute watches at a distance how all her companions fall happily into the arms of another woman after spending time with her. People with this wound feel they are here to heal others, and this leaves them feeling tremendously lonely with a fear of growing old. The Sacred Prostitute must be willing to release the wound of end-less service and open to personal one-on-one love with another. Sacred Prostitutes thrive on being in service, and it is precisely this quality they must be willing to release. When this wound is healed, more of their genuine gifts can burst forth. For it is in the act of true love/marriage that their dowry of inherited wisdom can be given.

The Magdalene Wound

The Magdalene wound is the fear and anguish of the beloved being torn away. Those with this wound have a feeling that should they meet their beloved in physical form, it will only be a matter of time before they are taken from them in some cruel way. They believe that they won't be together long enough, that their love is fated in some way. Or that their love is forbidden. When this wound is healed they won't care whether their heart gets broken, crushed, or bruised in any way; they will see this as a gift of loving. They will no longer hold back or delay the inevitable depths that they both could plunge to.

The Messiah Wound

The Messiah wound carries the endless and futile search for one's disci-ples. Those with this wound feel that their great work cannot come into fruition unless they have located and identified these followers. They feel unable to do/carry this alone. They feel troubled by this burden, and it heavily weighs them down. They are convinced that only when the twelve are present can the real magic begin. When this wound is healed they will realize that they are the Christ. That within them is the All, the Absolute, and the Only.

The ET Wound

The ET wound is the feeling of not belonging, of not understanding or having a sentimental connection to humanity, of feeling strangely lost and so far away from home. These people spend way too much time alone or holed up in a room, their head fixated on the computer. This results in a disconnection between mind and body, and maybe even a sense of wanting to discard the body. When this wound is healed they can own their origins with dignity and presence. It won't be something that has to be hidden or denied anymore, but celebrated and revered.

The Priest/Priestess Wound

The wound of the Priest/Priestess is the fear of persecution. The religious/pagan wars have left a huge scar upon these people's Soul, and its effects can be seriously paralyzing. Those that have this wound experience a battle inside of themselves. One part of them longs, needs, and is urging to practice once again, for the people and for the planet, while another part is locked in fear, terrified to connect and bring forth their sacred work. When this wound is healed, they will not fear the psychic underbelly of the patriarchy. They will be free.

The Twin Flame Wound

The Twin Flame wound is a feeling of either (a) having met one's Twin Flame and it failed miserably or (b) not being destined to meet their Twin Flame in physical form in this lifetime. Whichever one it is, there is this feeling of excruciating sadness and emotional death. Their heart feels like a wasteland, and it's a place on the inside they will utterly avoid at all costs. However, that place holds the key to their full reunion as it contains the root of their separation. When this wound is healed, they will be heading in the genuine direction of sacred union—a true merging and blending of seeming opposites. Their Twin Flame will arise, as will they. This realization will be lasting and timeless.

⚘ A Foundational Practice: Conscious Breathing

When we explore our sacred wounds, it can be unnerving. I suggest we always begin by first getting grounded and centered. This way if there are tough moments where we feel like we're becoming overwhelmed or lost, we have a reference point to return to, to get our bearings. This simple breathing practice is something I always turn to in times of personal grief and pain. It is universal because it begins and ends with breath. The three-part breath is taught in the yogic tradition but is inherent to the way in which we are intended to breathe. As we grow, learn, and hurt, we begin to absorb a strangulation and reversal of our breathing process. In some form or fashion, most of us adopt a reversal of breath. We begin to inhale and suck inward and breathe out and push our bellies out. Many, if not most of us, flip-flop breathe at some point in life. There are probably a lot of reasons why, but the many stresses begin to divert us from our natural breath and into a more constricted manner. For those who have experienced severe stress and trauma, this breath reversal is much more acute. In this way, we begin to feel breathless in much of life. Specifically, in trauma we either hold our breath or hyperventilate. To return to a relaxed place we must begin with the baseline of breath, the anchor of our life. Untethered, we float. Tethered, we are grounded and balanced from the inside out. Soothing and calming three-part breath is the simplest way to correct our learned breathing and return us to the breath of infancy.

1. Sit in a chair or lie down on your back—whatever is most comfortable.
2. Place your hands over your belly.
3. Inhale deeply and imagine that you are filling up your belly with air like a balloon.
4. Feel the balloon filling as your abdomen presses into your belly.
5. When your abdomen is full, pause for a moment then exhale out your nose or mouth.
6. After a few deep breaths, move your hands to your heart.
7. Take an even deeper breath, filling your lungs as your chest expands.
8. After a few deep breaths, move your hands to either side of your face.
9. Take an even deeper breath, filling your lungs, belly, rib cage, and chest like a wave rising until your lungs are full.
10. Release all the air in a sigh through your mouth.

11. Continue slowly for a few minutes, noticing what it feels like to increase the length of inhaled and exhaled breaths. I recommend using this breath practice whenever you feel anxious or triggered. Sometimes you will feel a shuddering in your belly as you breathe— this is the beginning of emotions rising to the surface. That's the time to keep going! Any moment now the shuddering will give way to buried feelings. It could be anger, fear, or sadness. Under all of that will be the grief, and this is what we are looking for. Grief is the only healing emotion; all the others are layers on the way down to sadness.

Canned Hunting

This sorrow of the world was written by and used with permission of Linda Tucker, white lion conservationist and CEO and founder of the Global White Lion Protection Trust. It is based on information she wrote for the Global White Lion Protection Trust website but has been adapted for this book. You can find out more about Linda's work and the conservation of white lions at the Global White Lion Protection Trust website and the Linda Tucker Foundation website.

A canned hunt is a trophy hunt in which an animal is kept in a confined, fenced-in area, increasing the likelihood of the hunter obtaining a kill. The hunter is then able to shoot the animal at point blank range for an agreed-upon price.

Canned hunting takes place for white lions on a regular basis. Below is a brief chronology from the Global White Lion Protection Trust, a leadership organization that has been the front-runner in campaigning against this killing industry for over three decades and, more importantly, is still a leader in pioneering protected status for lions:

From the 1960s until today, white lions were forcibly removed from their natural endemic habitat of Timbavati into cages, magic shows in the United States, zoos and circuses around the globe, and worse, factory farms that started breeding tame lions for killing.

In 1997, these illicit activities, which were undertaken by a mafia-like network, were exposed by the British investigative TV program *The Cook Report* and labelled "Canned Lion Hunting," i.e., lions in a can. What began as a mafia industry of trade in gunrunning, animal parts, and live animals became a tourist attraction, now offering a cub-petting experience. At first, a prohibition was put on these activities, but then in 2010, the South African High Court ruled *in favor of* the killing industry. From there, the international lion crisis escalated.

By 2014, people around the world were protesting this inhumane treatment of lions and the Global White Lion Protection Trust helped mobilize a Global March for Lions. Conservation groups worldwide united behind this cause and 1.5 million signatures were presented to the South African parliament. Unfortunately, all these efforts were ignored.

One year later, in 2015, the outrage at the killing of the white lion Cecil went viral, when Walter Palmer made world headlines for luring a wild lion out of a national park and then paying to be able to shoot it for "fun" with a crossbow. But this killer-dentist was not alone. At this time, in 2015, the United States was already responsible for more than 60 percent of the dead lions leaving Africa for canned hunts of this nature. Unfortunately, Walter Palmer's action of killing a wild lion pales in comparison with what's continuing to happen to captive lions today.

Today, *there are more lions in cages than in the wild*. South Africa, in particular, holds thousands of lions in captivity to serve a multimillion-dollar cuddle-and-kill industry. I know it's hard to believe, but please don't shut your hearts down. This lucrative, big cat production line first offers baby cubs to tourists to pet (for a price, of course), then offers these *same* tamed lions as adults to commercial trophy hunters to kill for an astronomical fee. You could easily be one of those tourists, happily hugging a lion cub, and thinking it's okay to do so. But what you need to know is that hugging a baby lion is a death sentence for the lion, and ultimately for all of us.

Here's the story for lions in this horrific industry: A few days after the lion cub is born, it's taken from its mother. As the mother thinks she has lost her cubs, she will almost immediately come back into estrus (or back into heat), as her sole purpose is for breeding for the trophy hunting outfitter she belongs to. She spends her whole life giving birth and having her cubs ripped away from her, and she never gets the chance to be a mother. Once her body is useless and can no longer have cubs she is either offered to be shot for a bargain price or thrown in for free as part of another hunt.

When the cub is taken from its mother it is sent to a petting zoo or a volunteer project, where tourists pay to interact with the cubs. This is very distressing for the cubs who have no means of getting away. Lions are nocturnal, and are designed to sleep during the day, cubs especially, but they are forced to be awake and handed from tourist to tourist for "selfies." When the cubs become too big for petting, they can be used again for tourists demanding a walking experience with lions, which provides further profits for lion outfitters and tourist destinations.

When that same tame lion is fully grown, it then comes time for the lion to be shot, so it is released into a small enclosure. The hunters are generally driven around the enclosure, on the back of open vehicles, looking for the tame, hand-raised lions, which now have no fear of humans and will often come extremely close to the vehicle. Meat is often hung out and the hunters open fire once the lion "takes the bait" and begins to eat. This way of shooting is also called "put and take." Often the tame lion feels it has freedom for the first time in its life, released from a cage, and as it sees the hunters approach it glances over and glances away, as it does not see humans as a threat. The cowards open fire and take pleasure in watching the bewildered animal roll around in agony and then watch the life drain out of its body. Sometimes it takes days of agony before the lion dies of its wounds. Videos of these canned hunts are shocking and horrifying. To the average person this is abhorrent, but to these hunters it's a mere sport.

Afterward, the dead lion is often paraded for ridiculous photos as the "big, brave" hunters stand over the lifeless corpse of a tame lion. They then return home to their countries to tell tales of how they killed a large and dangerous man-eating lion. They don't mention they killed a tame and often starving lion inside an enclosed area.

Trophy hunting outfits have now found another way to profit from the lions they kill: they sell lion bones to the Asian medicine market. This is the same market that has wiped many species off the face of the planet and is the biggest threat to tigers and rhinoceros today.

The other side of the coin of the killing industry is the cuddle industry where volunteers and tourists pay thousands of dollars to work on these types of projects with the promise that these cubs will one day be released. Unfortunately, the reality of the situation is that these cubs will never be released into the wild and that their destiny is to become a trophy for sport. Volunteers are led to believe they are doing a good thing when in fact what they're doing is helping to sustain an industry that is inhumane. We would strongly recommend that all volunteers do their homework. Any cub petting facility will most likely be providing lions for the canned hunting industry. Please use websites such as Volunteers in Africa Beware and do the research necessary to ensure that you're not unknowingly supporting this industry.

In October 2016, the Global White Lion Protection Trust presented to parliaments and submitted letters of objection to this burgeoning industry, launching a global campaign and amassing a petition of nearly 1.5 million signatures by the international advocacy group Avaaz demanding its prohibition. Many conservation groups united behind this cause, some referring to it as the "blood lions" industry.

However, in 2016, the Convention for the International Trade in Endangered Species ignored these appeals and legalized the notorious lion bone trade. Doing so increased wild lion hunting demand and put wild lion populations in South Africa at greater risk by downlisting the conservation status of lions in the country from "vulnerable" to "least concern." Over 800 lions are sent as carcasses out of the country, legally, to feed this seemingly bottomless industry.

What Can Be Done?

The Global White Lion Protection Trust has been actively campaigning against the canned hunting industry since the 1990s. In the midst of a global lion crisis that treats Africa's most sacred animals as a killing commodity in cross-border trade, founders of this nonprofit organization, Linda Tucker and special lion ecologist Jason A. Turner, have dedicated their lives to finding the solution.

In 2000, Linda Tucker embarked on a complicated strategy to rescue a white lion cub from one of these death camps. Its parents had been stolen from the wilds of Timbavati. Together with her partner Jason and a team of specialists, they returned the lion and her cubs to the wild in 2006. This return included a highly challenging long-term scientific reintroduction strategy that helped pioneer the way for similar efforts worldwide.

Where governments have failed, the Global White Lion Protection Trust has raised millions of dollars to establish a protected area for this iconic animal in the heart of its spiritual and ecological homelands, a United Nations biodiversity hotspot. Linda Tucker's life and work has been focused on campaigns to protect the white lions as a *living* heritage and restore them to their ancestral heartlands after more than six decades of forced removals rendered them all but extinct in their endemic habitat.

In 2004, when their StarLion project began, this ecocultural program united youth with elders, science with sacred spirituality, and modern technology with ancient wisdom to help restore human systems alongside ecosystems. Linda Tucker has also established a LionHearted Leadership model offering hope for a positive outcome not only for lions but for those humans who value their future as well.*

After reading these words from Linda Tucker, pause here for reflection. Take the time that is needed to truly be with these insights and understandings. Just breathe and be with them. Let's bear witness to the sobriety of the situation and feel one another as we rise together to receive more of Her transmission.

Let's move on without answers.

We must learn to trust the process, remembering that *this is an initiation.*

---

*Written by Linda Tucker based on material she wrote for the Global White Lion Protection Trust, adapted by Linda for this book.

FIVE
Standing Our Ground

There are a thousand things which prevent a woman from awakening, which keep her in the power of her dreams. In order to act consciously with the intention of awakening, it is necessary to know the nature of the forces which keep a woman in a state of sleep. First of all, it must be realized that the sleep in which a woman exists is not normal but hypnotic sleep. The woman is hypnotized, and this hypnotic state is continually maintained and strengthened in her. One would think that there are forces for whom it is useful and profitable to keep a woman in a hypnotic state and prevent her from seeing the truth and understanding her position.

G. I. GURDJIEFF

IN THIS CHAPTER, WE'RE GOING TO EXPLORE the unearthed potential that lurks in our hidden depths and develop the courage to bring it up, out, and into our communities.

I believe each and every one of us involved in this radical wave of awakening has within their grasp an edgy, innovative, and powerful gift for the world. Not as some kind of branding or marketing exercise that explodes upon our Facebook feeds as the latest "must-have" item but as a true and genuine enlightening experience that produces real and lasting change.

This sacred gift that I am speaking of shall become the good and solid ground that we shall be building upon for the duration of this book. To take this journey as deep and wide as we're able to, we're going to have to turn ourselves inside out and live from that truth. First, we must search for this sacred gift, and the way we do that is to start asking some uncomfortable and awkward questions in ever-increasing depth.

THE FIRST QUESTION IS: ARE WE FREE?

Are we physically free and able to move, travel, connect, network, share, speak, give, and receive? Or is there some kind of petty tyrant—internal or external—that attempts to prevent our gathering and connecting with others? If there is, we need to address this properly.

We must be sure to examine our own internal mechanisms. Do we hold ourselves back from sharing and gathering? Do we shy away from connecting with others? Do we leave it to other people to dream up ideas, organize a gathering, attend the gathering, and then implement those ideas into action? Are we sitting on the fence in some way, watching others get involved and wishing we were part of it?

One of the greatest threats to the Dark Agenda is the gathering of people, coming together with a shared passion and then brought into a heightened state of wakefulness. This high-level inspiration and elevation is highly feared and not encouraged in any way by the everyday invisible laws of society. Sometimes I wonder whether man-made substances are brought into our cultures on purpose, to make sure we don't figure out how to reach those states by ourselves. Because if we do, we won't work for a low wage, we won't commute in dirty fuel-driven transportation into the toxic haze of urban sprawl, and we won't go home to square boxes that cramp our spirit and break down our creativity and intimacy.

No, instead we will be outdoors, sitting by fires, playing and creating in our fervent, green, tangled crazy natural home, where we are no longer "safe," but dancing.

In this day and age, there cannot be an inner or outer perpetrator that controls our freedom to gather, share, and participate. We must examine our relationships in deep and honest ways, including the relationship we have with ourselves. We must check in and ask, "Is anything attempting to hold me back in any way? Am I, or is someone/thing, keeping what I currently offer in the safe confines of popularity, 'brandability,' and financial security?"

Now is not the time for safe and credible creativity. Now is the time for new, edgy, and innovative ideas and experiments and creative, spiritual initiations that provide authentic and lasting growth. We must stop appealing to the popularity vote and take that extra step into vast unknown parts of ourselves, asking "What more can I give?" which also answers the more egoic focused question of "What more can I receive?"

Let us stop branding ourselves on Instagram and Facebook like some kind of product placement that thrives on appearance. Please let us stop typing up posts that get the most "likes" and go viral because they are glamorous, sexy, or outrageous in some way. Let us stop prostituting ourselves for an invisible world that doesn't actually exist and relies upon our addictive and narcissistic nature to not only survive but thrive. The reason I'm writing this is because I have done this myself. I didn't realize it consciously of course, but I was making myself into a brand! I was becoming a perfect patriarchy puppet. A pleasing, loving, fence-sitter that was popular, sellable, and safe.

It was thanks to Andrew Harvey, and the time I spent with him and Linda Tucker at the Global White Lion Protection Trust in South Africa, that began to change all of this for me. He backed the group of us there into a tight and restricted corner, asking us horribly uncomfortable questions, such as "Why do you think you have received mystical experiences? What are you doing during this time as the world burns in agony because of your incessant greed and entitlement?" And then, the final bludgeon, "What's more frightening? Being numb with apathy as you sip yet another glass of chardonnay as the last tree on the planet burns to the ground, or allowing your veins to be filled with the fire of Kali, protesting with your 'No!' and wakefulness during the destruction of your planet and your possible extinction?"

Gulp.

After tremendous waves of shock, disgust, and desolation I eventually shook my head in disbelief and decided then and there that I desperately needed to get the courage to show up in ways that at first terrified me and then later inspired me.

So on that electrifying note, let's use our online presence to write the kinds of things that will genuinely assist others and encourage ourselves to be more outspoken and authentic. Let's encourage one another's honest, beauty, and transparency. Let's bring joy and catalyzing possibility to our posts.

Now, let's return to our sacred gift. In essence, its discovery is a win-win situation, even if it does not initially appear to be that way. To access it, we will be stretched beyond our comfort zones. Surrounding this sacred gift, otherwise known as an evolutionary game changer, will be three frightening guardians whose job it is to keep us from discovering our sacred gift, our sacred technology if you will. These three guardians will attempt to sway us in an entirely different direction by appealing to our vanity, fear, and cowardice. Only the brave of heart will refuse to listen or run away from their terrible threats and appearances. If they strike at our vanity, we will crumble as we imagine all the judgmental things people could say about us, and how unpopular we could become. We will worry about not being liked or celebrated as we usually are, and so we might back down and turn away—never to be seen again. Should these three guardians strike at our fear, we will be paralyzed at all the awful things that could happen to us, like being hunted or persecuted for doing or saying the wrong thing, and thereby venture no further. Or if they strike at our cowardice we will feel unworthy and unable to challenge their alleged superiority and stay like we've always been—impotent, weak, and malleable.

However, should we continue past these three, choosing to see and hear the deepest mystical part of ourselves, and decide to go into our communities no longer holding anything back—what would that look like? This is the question that now needs answering.

The Fierce Feminine is not deterred by danger or pain. She is not put off by other people's opinions. She is not prepared to water down, dilute, or appease anyone or anything for Her presence to reach those that it must and bring about the balance that is so desperately needed.

There are many of us on the path of sacred activism, acting on behalf of the Fierce Feminine, who will, at certain times, be challenged to a greater call of duty. Standing our ground has nothing to do with being stubborn, nothing to do with being stupid, and nothing to do with being naïve. Standing our ground is when we take a firm stance as a sovereign being who is free and will not allow anyone to breach our boundaries and tamper with our Light, or the Light of others.

Standing our ground is not easy, but it is necessary. It requires a certain fortitude internally as well as externally. We must be prepared to be bombarded by the forces of anti-awakening; doubt, dread, despair, disillusionment, and questioning whether we ought to back down will arise.

In these moments we must be *awake* to what's happening by declaring to that which attempts to ensnare us, "I am a sovereign being. I am free. I am one with my True Creator. I am not afraid of you anymore. I am protecting my Light."

It is then that we will feel a change of atmosphere within, and a lightness will be seen and felt. From there, we can send this glorious peace into the epicenter of the swirling dark fog (both inner and outer).

Remember, beloved friends, standing our ground is not about being defiant or aggressive but about being firm and fearlessly truthful. We can hand over all our fears and doubts to our God and rest in the great knowledge that we are taking this stance for more than just ourselves; we are doing it for each other and our Earth.

ARE WE COWARDS?

Fear. There's something honest about it. It's a shutdown. It's a no. We're simply unable to move forward in these moments of fear. It's a true paralysis, a real situation. Whereas cowardice is a choice to not act when we know we can. A coward knows they can reach for a certain action, knows they have the firepower (or compassion) to say what needs to be said, knows they *could* contribute to a situation that is clearly, obviously crying out for assistance—and instead walks away. I know this because I have been a coward. And I suspect many of us are or have been cowards in this lifetime.

> *Cowardice asks the question: "Is it safe?" Expediency asks the question: "Is it politic?" Vanity asks the question: "Is it popular?" But conscience asks the question: "Is it right?" And there comes a time when one must take a position that is neither safe, nor politic, nor popular but one must take it because one's conscience tells one what is right.*
>
> MARTIN LUTHER KING, JR.

A coward is someone who runs away or abandons their responsibilities or obligations during times of danger, distress, pain, or fear of the unknown; a coward is someone whose concern is only for themselves. Cowardice is a sickness, and it's rife among humans. I feel it's positively encouraged by the Dark Agenda to be a coward. I feel we are fed a program of cowardice-making propaganda. Examples of this include the following:

"Don't do this, or you'll get arrested."

"Don't do this, or you'll get sent to jail."

"Don't do this, or you'll have your car, home, job, child, land taken away."

"Don't do this, or we'll send the bailiffs, police, lawyers."

"Don't do this, or daddy (i.e., the system) is going to scold you."

"Don't do this, or mommy (i.e., the earth via natural disaster) will be angry."

And so we back down, become small, and hope to God no one punishes us.

We must stop this. We must stop being cowards and start being courageous. Courage doesn't mean we are fearless. It means we move forward despite, and maybe because of, our fear. We do it anyway. We take that giant leap, we respond to the call of duty and we act, speak up, go out on a limb, and claim our ability to do something that may frighten us, but we do it for all. We toss our concerns of being judged or ostracized or upsetting people's feelings as far away from us as we can. Because if it's a real situation, a real Fierce Feminine call to duty, if people and animals are getting hurt, land is being poisoned, or a pipeline is planned to go through sacred lands, then hurting other people's feelings is completely unimportant. The ones sitting on the fence will be the first to judge. Those who gossip are never empowered; it's always the ones who are afraid of threatening the status quo who lash out. You may become ostracized, slandered, blamed, and shamed but remember, these are the impotent cries of the cowards. The ones who know they can act and still decide not to.

We must reach for our courage. Let's reject the cowardice propaganda program and with a full, brave heart celebrate our daily acts of courage.

WHAT NEXT STEP
ARE WE CURRENTLY DENYING?

By now we should be getting a sense of an invigorating urgency that's seeping into our bones and filling us with inspiration and activation. Come with me and let's walk to the precipice of our currently comfortable-ish life and look beyond. What unknown horizon can we see that we sense deep down we could inhabit if only we took that new and unknown step? Take into consideration all the bullshit, fakery, control, and otherworldly interference that is tampering with our right to thrive harmoniously on this planet. If we imagine the knife edge we're on—what would be our next level of contribution to the world? In this exercise, let's genuinely reach for the extra mile and bravely shine the Light of our consciousness into our dark and yet unformed matter, asking ourselves the question, "What is my next level of contribution?"

> I'm an educator; what more could I teach?
>
> I'm a facilitator of sacred arts; what greater depth could I guide my participants into?
>
> I'm a healer; what new dimension could I work on?
>
> I'm a writer; what trailblazing words could be my legacy?
>
> I'm a speaker/performer; what excruciatingly raw, new depth could I transmit from?
>
> I'm in business; what innovative "green" product/service could I sell/offer?

These are dangerous questions to ask ourselves because our inner wisdom is only too happy to reply.

⚚ Sacred Action

Come into a comfortable lying-down position with your feet flopped open and your palms face up. Take this time to disengage from the exterior world, leaving behind all your worries, daily concerns, and thoughts and feelings concerning others. Come into yourself. Use your breath to transport your awareness from "out there" to inside yourself. Feel your familiar inner space and rest there awhile in the dark warmth of your sovereign being.

Start to see the natural world, the animal kingdom, the flora and fauna, the rivers, mountains, forests, and deserts. Feel the goodness of life and the innocent and delicate ways we depend on one another. Now, see the matrix—the artificial world of control, fear, otherworldly influences, war, and oppression. See how the matrix attempts to overlay the natural world, dimming the beauty of life from our vision. Coercing us into a world of impossible goals, unmet expectations, and a complete inability to open, trust, and connect.

What does She, the Fierce Feminine, have to say about that?

Should you allow this in, what next step could you take to fully contribute on behalf of Her authentic voice? What deep wisdom rests in your bones? What daring new dimension could you operate on? What innovative and fresh new territory could you guide others into? How else could something come through you, and what would it be?

Remember, Her way is not to oppose the Dark Agenda but to bring it into balance with nature.

Once you have seen your next new step, you must write it down. Better still, speak it to another (or record your own voice speaking Her words). Don't discard it or forget what you have been shown. This glimpse is between you and Her and has been revealed by your own wisdom. She has prepared and opened your evolution and will bring you every resource needed along the way.

And that is the Truth.

*There is a difference between knowing the path
and walking the path.*

Transmission
Summoning the Fecund Fierce Feminine*

Come into a comfortable lying-down position with your feet flopped open, your palms face up, and your eyes closed as you gaze into your being. Use this time to come into a more relaxed and open state. Begin to elongate your breath as you sink into and merge with your interior Self. Drop into the warm embrace that is familiar, recognizable, and true. It is always there for you, always welcoming and always beckoning.

---

*An audio track of this meditative exercise can be downloaded at audio.innertraditions .com/fiferi.

We are now going to journey with the fecund feminine; that earthy green, wild, unruly, natural force that pushes flowers up through the earth, that causes rosebuds to open, that turns the sunflower to face the light. Imagine yourself now in one of your most familiar, sacred sites, and there's no one else there. You feel safe, you feel held, you are not being overlooked. You are completely and gorgeously alone, and it feels Divine to you.

Remembering now the words a shaman once uttered to me: "Nature shall remember Her own." If we are one of Her own, then we will feel as She feels. In this transmission, let us throw off our human identity and become more like the one who created our body of Her own elements. She sustains our body out of Her own breath and shall take our body when it is time for this earthly end. And this taking can be just as ecstatic as the birthing.

Keep dropping, breath by breath, merging, longing for . . .

Here and now, before Earth and sky, we feel the blessing of your infinite love in our bones, in our blood, in our breath, and in our hearts.

As you rest in the presence of prayer imagine that the earth you find yourself lying upon begins to grow small, delicate tendrils that now wriggle and climb up your toes. You can feel this as tiny cords and threads, emerald green in nature, twirling up like ivy against a wall. You can feel this tickling underfoot, as this moist, mossy, green tangled wildness starts to climb up and draws you in. You're sure there's a quality of energy that is knowingly enticing, knowingly climbing in such a way that brings in delight—you can feel it.

And of course you wonder, where is that intention coming from? What is that intention coming from? And it is the good heart of nature. The good heart of nature that is free of all interpretation. The good heart of nature that is simply pure goodness; it brings pleasure, it brings delight, it brings laughter, it brings joy, and it squeals and rasps. It is unapologetic, not holding back in any way, continuing to climb despite your flapping. By now it's carefully carving its way up the back of your calves and shins. Your feet are completely submerged in the earth, and it is warm and it is not at all uncomfortable. The soles of your feet are picking up on a pulse, a rhythm. You can feel the life force pounding in the moist earth, as the ivy continues to climb in such a way that surprises and delights you. It continues to climb past your knees, now along your thighs. You are letting go, there is most definitely a sense of sensuality, more than anything you've ever experienced with another fellow human. There is a great skill being applied here, a great know-how.

The ivy that is climbing you made *you. It knows, because you are made of it. It knows how to awaken your flesh. It is warm and excites your blood. Years and years of disappointed love affairs slide from your being because this presence knows, this presence is the Creatrix. It is barely bearable, almost half a breath away from being too much. There is no part of your body that is receiving more attention than another. The whole of your body is being inundated with natural, knowledgeable presence as the tendrils climb into your groin, around your behind, between your legs, over your pubic bone, toward your sexual center—there is no confusion here. It is all one and the same.*

Try to keep the mind clear here and permit the sensations. Climbing up and over the buttocks this energy goes, weaving its way up and over the sexual center, toward the sacrum. Pure wise know-how.

The tendrils are only claiming their own, taking back what is being freely given, and they continue to climb over the naval, over the stomach, kidneys, lower back, into the coccyx, into the spinal cord making their way up through the hollow of the spine, weaving up and over each vertebra. Coming to the base of the breasts, and with such delicate, green fingers climbing, claiming the breasts. Delighting around the fullness of the breasts, nipples, and armpits.

Crawling up the upper back and in between the shoulder blades. Getting underneath the shoulder blades and into the gap under the ribs, coming into the voice, claiming the arms, neck, throat, jaw, mouth, teeth, tongue, eyes, third eye, scalp, brain, and the stem of the brain.

Taken. Taken. Taken.

Green, fecund, feminine is everywhere.

You breathe and are as one.

See yourself spread-eagled as it were, as her green chlorophyll pours through your veins and arteries. Your mind belongs to nature.

From here, imagine that you come to your feet. And you are being called by Her to a very barren part of the natural world. You are being drawn to where it's extremely dry, empty, cut down, draught-ridden, infected, and scorched.

And you are walking through this, as barefoot as She is. You are that young, green, fertile, fecund, moist beauty. You are walking through parts of nature that are struggling to survive and the whole thing is very sensual. You are totally embracing burned and charred trees. You are holding trunks as if they were your beloved. You are breathing, sounding those earthly sounds, as you kiss the struggling trees. Every footstep is laced with an enticing beckoning to come back to life. As you walk, you continue to delight yourself by rubbing the backs of your fingers up your skin. The wind plays with you, circles around you, finding those places that bring more of She into you. The wind is keeping you constantly on the edge of ecstatic pleasure but is not a pleasure for yourself, it is a pleasure for this struggling piece of earth that you are vivifying, rejuvenating, restoring.

You show all of yourself to the natural world. There are no parts of you that are shamed or hidden; you are loving the whole of your body. And because you have been taken by the fecund feminine there is no human program whispering in your head as to what is appropriate and what is not. Your noble task is to seep into this struggling earth and turn it over so that it can be reborn and awakened.

Always, always, always just on the bearable edge of ecstasy, and you may be lost completely. You are just about here. Aligning with your noble cause. You sing into the lakes, and the pools, and the springs. You reach into the dried-up springs and unclutter them, pull from the source of water until they flow again. You are right up to your elbows, sometimes your shoulders as you rummage around inside of the spring, clearing it completely, as your fingertips call for the source of water to come. And it comes.

It comes, and it comes, and it comes.

When it pours out of the earth with a pulse, you can feel the joy of it, the ecstasy of it, you can even feel the peace of it.

As you look behind you, in your wake is beauty—you see new shoots, new buds, new earth, and the beginnings of growth. And this excites you. You dance and you swirl and you turn and you twirl and you arch. You beckon and gather and sew and weave. Nature shall remember Her own.

And you are remembering.

✦·✦

Battery Farms

The film *Land of Hope and Glory* reveals the truth about battery farms as well:

> Ninety percent of chicken production in the UK is indoors with the birds kept in extremely cramped sheds, which usually house anywhere between 20 to 50 thousand chickens each. Placed in the sheds after birth, the chickens will never leave the barns until the day they die. The chickens are kept under near constant dim artificial light as this is believed to increase feed intake and maximizes growth in chickens.
>
> Due to selective breeding and genetic modification, the birds reach slaughter age in just forty-one days, in essence meaning that they are chicks in an obese, adult body as at forty-one days old in the wild the chicks would still be sheltering under their mother's

wings. . . . Due to the incredibly fast rates of growth birds raised for meat suffer terribly, their young bones unable to support them, breaking under the weight and strain of their disfigured bodies, resulting in painful lameness, which prevents them from eating, drinking, or even standing up. . . .

When the birds have reached slaughter age, they are transported to their deaths. Teams of catchers work at high speeds to load up huge transport lorries, violently grabbing the birds and flinging them into crates. Due to the heavy-handed and fast-paced operation, many of the animals have their legs and wings broken, their skulls crushed, and their hips dislocated. This results in the birds being forced to endure relentless pain on their journey to slaughter.

The birds are transported in tiny crates, creating an extremely stressful environment with no access to food or water.

This is the first time the birds will feel sunlight or breathe fresh air. . . .

Those that make it alive to the slaughterhouse are then shackled by their feet and hung upside down. After they have been shackled, they are then carried to an electric water bath, where they will suffer a painful electrical shock thats purpose is to render them unconscious. However, many of the birds do not get stunned as they do not make contact with the water and some regain consciousness before they reach the neck cutter, meaning that these birds are fully conscious as their throats are sliced open.*

I have seen inside a battery farm, and these birds do not resemble the chickens we like to associate with farmyards. Even before I entered, I knew what I was about to see would haunt me for the rest of my life, and it does.

---

*Land of Hope and Glory, created by the founders of animal rights organization Surge with research and editing done by Ed Winters and Luna Woods, 2017, Land of Hope and Glory: UK Animal Farming website. You can find a full list of the public investigations featured in the film on the website as well as additional facts and references.

It is a disgrace.

Pause here for reflection. Take the time that is needed to truly be with these insights and understandings. Just breathe and be with them. Let's bear witness to the sobriety of the situation and feel one another as we rise together to receive more of Her transmission.

Let's move on without answers.

We must learn to trust the process, remembering that *this is an initiation*.

SIX
Sovereign Sexuality

This dance is a prayer. A prayer for the earth, and therefore a prayer for women. This is a call for women to know and believe in the holiness of their bodies, the sacredness of their dance, and the power of their voice. A prayer for all women who do not express themselves, who hold themselves back, who do not know their own power as Creators, as Healers, as Givers of Life. My prayer is a prayer for women; women who are not allowed to dance and sing, or express themselves in any way. A prayer for men who do not believe women should dance in public. My dance is the voice of women who are trapped in a life where they have no voice. My prayer is for the young girls who get sold into marriage at eight years old to old men, and who die in the hands of cultures that permit such atrocities to continue . . . and continue . . . My prayer is for young girls who are sold into sex slavery and contract illnesses they didn't even know existed. My prayer is for these girls who never had a chance to be girls. My prayer is for the men whose unpunished violence and terror against women and against the earth is permitted in this world. My prayer is a dance for the earth. My prayer is a dance for women. My prayer is a calling for the women to Return to the Temple.

ZOLA DUBNIKOVA, FROM HER WEBSITE OF THE
SAME NAME (YOU CAN ALSO FIND HER ON FACEBOOK
AT ZOLA DUBNIKOVA—HOLISTIC DANCE LANGUAGE)

BELOVED FRIENDS, NOW WE GET TO SHINE the Light of consciousness over our sexuality and the kinds of partners we have been and perhaps are still choosing to be. In earlier chapters, we delved deep into our being for the highest offering that could be made through us and into our communities, a gift that has been truly given and is ours to share. It is a rarity for us to be able to see this, let alone be in a position to be able and willing to implement it. This treasure trove dwells in our root; therefore, any energy that enters us sexually will either inspire and elevate our sacred gift or diminish and dampen it down.

It's not so much the partner or the person that does this, but rather it's the energy that is running through them that has this impact. It is the resonance, the vibration and frequency of the person's usual state of being that can heal or hinder. Without a developed emotional intelligence and a trusted intuitive awareness, we become easy targets for the Dark Agenda to end the potential awakening found within all genuine loving relationships. Emotional intuitive intelligence also helps us to become more discerning with regard to whom we engage with, especially on intimate and sexual levels.

When we discover what we are capable of birthing in the world and we bring in a partner that is afraid of that gift and what we could become should we actualize it, then that partner will not be able to keep themselves from being an agent of foreign influence that seeks to diminish our gifts.

However, if we are with a partner who does not fear this unprecedented feminine force and all we could become, but instead rejoices at this exciting potential, then this partner will be nothing but supportive, encouraging, and inspired—a source of sustenance for all that could come through us.

THE DAY A WOMAN OPENED ME

A few years ago I became familiar with a traveling Tantrika who was living in my area in a quiet and unassuming way. People spoke of how she walked barefoot in the mountains with only water and chia seeds for sustenance. Her discipline impressed me, and for a moment I wondered whether our paths would cross.

As the weeks passed, news of this woman continued to reach my ears. Some described her as being a woman of the earth, grounded and natural looking. They said she was incredibly comfortable in her skin and did not appear or behave in a way one would imagine given her line of work.

This news spurred me on. If I was going to approach such a person, her presence was presenting itself in such a way that whispered "she is the one" in my ear.

I gathered the nerve to contact her, to reach out and ask for her time. I had no definitive reason for why I was calling on her. It was simply an inner knowing that this was going to happen. It seemed as if our Souls had prearranged our meeting, and all we had to do was show up.

The first time, I canceled. I backed out. I was afraid of what this could mean, and where it might lead. I had to be even more sure that she was 100 percent trustworthy, and more importantly, that I could trust myself. I had to know that I would keep myself safe and speak out if I felt things were going astray.

The second time, I kept our agreement.

Sure enough, just as I was told, she was a woman of the earth. No makeup, no goddess clothes, no sexy energy. She was natural. She was relaxed. And she knew exactly where I was, and where I wanted to go.

I explained that I needed our encounter with one another to be in alignment with my Soul and how integrity and skill were of the highest importance. I asked for a vertical experience, something that would open me to the unknown. I explained that this wasn't about sex or orgasms or how to become a better lover. I simply needed to know how much more my body could open. I needed to know what was possible and whether all these ecstatic states were merely a myth.

She smiled with such peace that I instantly settled and opened to what was to come. She knew about breath. She knew about rhythm.

She knew about pressure. She knew about prayer. She knew about body locks and mudras. And she knew about God.

She kneaded me, stroked me, slid up and down me, activated my spine, expanded my breath capacity, she gave me permission to let go. She gave me permission to awaken to the earthly forces contained within my body, and at the last moment catapult them into the glittering, ecstatic whirlpool of my quivering and anticipating spirit.

She explained how she saw my body as an hourglass, and that her one and only intention was to turn my energy upside down.

In those last and explosive moments, I felt like a pinball being shot to the top of the game, that place where you light everything up and your score goes through the roof!

She catapulted me three times. One for the body, one for the heart, and one for the Soul.

Then there was only white Light.

Expansion.

Fluidity.

Gossamer thin veils being lifted,

and more Light,

and more Light,

and more Light . . . and then

Silence. Deafening silence.

Then, somewhere in the distance, I could hear a gentle, tiny voice. Saying over and over again, "Thank you, thank you, thank you."

Soon, I realized that it was me. I was on my side in the fetal position, rocking myself back and forth speaking to everything and everyone, but especially her, and especially me.

So yes, I can categorically say with my hand on my heart, bodies open to reveal the spirit within. There is a way to do this, and it doesn't have to be overtly sexual or icky, and you don't have to hand over your power. There is a skilled and highly conscious application of being able to do this with integrity at its core. And this is something this woman is going to pass on to me at the time of this writing.

For me, this experience was and is in the number one spot in terms of spiritual epiphanies. It showed me what is possible and where I can now lean in. It encourages me to open, way past the usual stopgaps with a man. This woman gave me the space to find myself in the sexual realm and show me that spirit can lead the way.

My utmost and sincere prayer is for my husband Pete to experience this too. I know he has been here because of the plant medicines he has taken. But how wondrous it would be to experience this together and to help others to find this place too.

We must be incredibly discerning about who comes into our temple, as only those who are worthy can and should enter our temple doors. The yogis tell us that the female is more receptive to the incoming penetrative quality of the male. However, she isn't designed to keep on taking in all his projections, emotions, and astral and mental energy without maintaining her own good health and cleanliness.

But of course, we have almost forgotten all these yogic philosophies. These ancient healing practices have become lost over time, and the female has continued to clog herself up with the energetics that get transmitted through the sexual act. Thankfully, all of this is now being remembered and exchanged in widespread women's circles and literature across the world.

My one concern is that it's only being read and not acted upon. Not only do we need to be discerning and aware of our partner's emotional, mental, and intellectual vibration when we come together in the act of love, but we also must be aware of the environment that we are making love in. To avoid attracting and feeding the paranormal virus as it attempts to infect the living cells of our love relationships, we must start with emotional intelligence. Pent-up emotions and unhealed wounds can cause tension, anger, and depression and act as a magnetic attractor to more of the same. It is the same for the environment. What is the quality of the space that we are making love in? What memories lurk there? How does this environment make us feel—at ease or uptight?

Developing emotional awareness and intelligence means being willing to be present with our feelings and needs, respecting others and engaging in mindfulness practices. Tracking our behavior patterns such as compulsions, addictions, and things that "trigger" us emotionally is essential to expanding our awareness. It's part of raising our consciousness and evolving as human beings. Once the awareness of unresolved emotions emerges, it is the responsibility of the more aware partner to address these issues and perhaps say no, for the moment.

So let's carry on and feel into what *our* sovereign sexuality is. Do we actually know? Perhaps, like me, you have been heavily conditioned by the Dark Agenda to be a certain way when it comes to sex. As a woman we are encouraged to seduce, thrill, and excite, whereas a man is led to believe that he must go out there and take what he wants and then own it.

Even the way we dress, behave, speak, and move has most probably been conditioned into us by the sex program deliberately dreamt up by the Dark Agenda to keep us addicted and distracted by a pastime that simply did not deliver, until now.

Let's end that program right here and now by pulling it up by its roots and vowing to stay awake when it comes to sex, and who and what we are saying yes to.

BAPTISM OF SHAKTI

Light and Dark Rivers

It is said that Mary Magdalene would baptize others into the faith at the confluence of two rivers. Baptizing in this way goes all the way back to pagan times. The meeting and merging of two rivers is a symbolic representation of what baptism means—the birth of a new being, forged from the alchemical fires of two seeming opposites, melded down into one unknown but familiar expression, outside of our dualistic understanding and cultural norm.

It's this kind of imagery that holds the key to understanding the greater task of merging the Light and Dark Rivers within ourselves.

When they meet and meld within, we are invoking the Baptism of Shakti. A fully liberated body, heart, and mind saturation of serpentine euphoria and pulsating vibrant presence.

But first, let's go back a few steps and learn what the Light and Dark Rivers truly are.

These "rivers" are meridians or nerve/Light channels of subtle energy also known as *nadis*. They carry, transport, and channel universal life force in and out of our physical and spiritual bodies.

The Light River channels a very soft, passive, tender, loving, innocent, gentle flow of life force, whereas the Dark River carries a richer, more voluptuous, pulsing, primordial, urgent flow of unchartered beingness through our subtle veins.

The Light and Dark Rivers can also be personified as Eve and Lilith, the good girl and the bad girl from the creation stories in the Old Testament in the Bible. Before we go any further we have to realize this good/bad girl understanding is a false construct dreamt up by the Dark Agenda. This split between Lilith and Eve is what we most need to heal in both man and woman. But to get there we will have to push past the church and their heavy doctrine, disregard and detach from the media and their "you have to be/look/act this way" dogma, and quite possibly move beyond our own judgment and fear.

Shakti is a word that describes the creative Divine presence of the feminine. You could say Shakti is the essence of vibrant health, feeling good in your own skin and feeling that your life has meaning and value.

Our task as women—and especially women who are opening to the Fierce Feminine—is to seek out the emergence of the Light and Dark Rivers within and to then share that not only with our beloved partners in the realm of intimacy but also as a representation and expression of whole women out in the world.

In the Western world, we often imagine that the Dark River, Lilith, is personified in pornography, prostitution, taboo sexual practices, and dark novels or movies. But this representation is not the Dark River; this is the Dark Agenda program of the Dark River. This is their love/hate relationship with the feminine. It is made up of pure fantasy and projection and laced with their distaste for their own creation. We on the other hand, under the influence of the Dark Agenda, have denied and suppressed our true connection with Her. Until we have retrieved and welcomed Her back into the fold, we will always know something important is missing.

The true Dark River or dark goddess emerges from the void. Preverbal, unknown, nameless, rhythmic, intelligent, and forward moving. A deep yearning that is willing to not know, willing to lose the grip of the mind and be transported into whatever is needed in the moment to serve the full glory of creation. Her essence holds the key to ignite, catalyze, reveal, and permit gnosis (direct knowing). This expression of the feminine is the medicine we most hunger for in this moment of our evolution. We are sick and tired of stasis, remaining the same and not getting anywhere. It is this Dark River that will demolish the false self, the inhibitions, the conditions placed upon us and the too small and too tight box we have lived in for most of our lives.

The Dark River as the Fierce Feminine holds open the door to our full potential and empowerment and urges us to take the extra step and reach for both.

The Dark River is the Fierce Feminine: sacred outrage and the most needed expression on the Earth at this time. She is unapologetic, brazen, bold, vastly intelligent, initiatory, and mesmerizing. But She does not harm any aspect of life; nor does She misrepresent, endanger, misinform, manipulate, or coerce the self or others. She lives outside of rules and order. Her outward action is the shattering of lies, denials, and illusion. Her inward actions are initiation, revelation, and authentic gnosis.

The Light River emerges from our sacred origins. She is exquisite tenderness, the sacred heart, purity, and virgin Light power. The Light River is not passive, weak, naïve, or ineffective. This again is the false understanding as taught to us by the patriarchy, or the Dark Agenda. Eve, or the Light River's true strength, flows within Her purity, Her absolute irrevocable union with what sustains, sources, and births at the most incandescent levels—that is Her virtue, Her faith and knowingness of Her own true nobility and elegance. She is graceful, dignified, compassionate, empathic, sacredly connected with all life, at peace, and filled with devotional bliss.

Her touch, glance, voice, and body soothe, soften, ease, and heal. Like the sweetest honey, the most refreshing spring water, She brings us new life, faith, and a restored vigor to join with life more than ever before. The Light River holds open the door to our pure vulnerability and quiet humility and encourages us to earnestly reach for them.

So when we imagine the authentic coming together of these two, well, I'm sure you can feel already what that promises to deliver. Together, their fusion births us into an entirely whole and new reality. Her outward action is the comforting of the Soul, the healing of all wounds, and the restoration of harmony on Earth. Her inward action is gentle guidance toward the heart, the softening of all that is rigid within and the restorer of trust, innocence, and immaculate sovereignty.

The Light River seduces our Soul, as She pours us into the secret Rumi heart, bringing us into contact with our unspeakable purity and worship as we drown in devotion to what we find there. The Dark River loosens up our mind, shakes off our masks, vivifies our sacred purpose, and makes real our Soul memories and our reason for being here. As the two rivers come into contact and merge in the psyche, the long-awaited union explodes the body, heart, and mind into a third and currently unknown new being. Something the Dark Agenda has feared for a very long time, but which we have patiently longed for.

SHIVA

The Glance of Truth

Let us now feel into the masculine principle at his ripest for sexual union. Amplified presence is his highest and most intoxicating extravagance toward the feminine, and his power is in his glance. That moment, that meeting of eyes between the lover and the beloved, invokes the ache of longing for reunion, where there exists not just the union of two Souls but the crux of the universe.

Shiva is the word that claims this moment. The free fall into Truth. The full-blown exposure of hungered-for obliteration as two become one. The mind, exploded into a million, billion pieces as the witness, drowning in love, gets to meet the beloved in an orgy of Absolute Truth. Shiva, the white Light; the be all and end all.

Shiva is the staggering presence of pure penetration, and there is no place that he is not. He has found you, and all eyes turn toward him. There is nothing other than this glance, happening in every moment, everywhere. Shiva is the full stop, the period. The abrupt and inconvenient Truth.

Eyes moist and wide with wonder, quivering, rasping breath, clamoring heart, levitating hairs, silence pounding through the ears, hanging on to our last bits of identity, he then takes another step closer into us and whispers, "I am here."

And we are gone.

Falling to our knees with arms outstretched and backs bent forward in imperative surrender, a sound escapes our lips, and it is the cry of our true name. The utterance of this holy seed spills upon the earth as redemptive blossoms that kiss and caress creation.

Shiva embodied. Our full-blown realization of I am. I am. I am.

Long exhale.

That is what we must aim and ask for.

CLEARING PAST RELATIONSHIPS

When a relationship ends, the woman is left carrying an impression of her lover in the energetics of her womb. Whenever the internal liquids between two merge, a transfer of energy—emotional and psychic—is passed and stored within the woman. Like a hall of records, this woman will continue to accumulate these energetic snapshots of her lovers until she brings her awareness to the kinds of rituals and practices that can clear and empty her of the past.

The kind of data that a woman will carry is the heart/body/Soul quality of the man in the moment of penetrative and/or oral sex, as well as in the moment of deep, meaningful kissing. These are the moments when the energetic transfer is made. And what is contained within that transfer is the vibrational quality of that man's physical body (is he well, vibrant, and fresh or stagnant, unhealthy, and "dis-eased"?), his emotional condition (is he open, loving, trusting, and innocent or angry, shut down, and withdrawn?), as well as his state of mind (is he present, clear-headed, and aware of what's happening or elsewhere planning or thinking about someone/thing else and/or confused?).

All of this information must be considered. And it's not only the partner's energies we absorb, but those of the environment we are in as well. Where are we making love? Is it a beautiful, clean sacred space when the time is our own, and our bodies are prepared and relaxed? Or is it someone else's space, someone else's bed strewn with their belongings and time is rushed because you fear someone returning?

The womb records all of this. And to clear this transfer we need to perform a ritual. Praying, meditating, or breathing it away is not enough; we need to involve a physical element to make it real and for a lasting healing to take place. For me, yoni eggs were the answer.

CLEARING THE WOMB AFTER LOVE

Yoni Eggs

Yoni eggs, also known as jade eggs or love eggs, are beautiful semi-precious stones carved into egg shapes and polished to be worn inside the yoni. I knew immediately, "Yes this is my practice." I have worked with crystals half of my life to heal, purify, activate, and amplify, so to insert one into my yoni seemed like the most natural and authentic way for me to heal these energetic transfers.

Yoni is the Sanskrit word for the female genitalia that means "sacred space." Its symbol has been worshipped in Eastern cultures since ancient times for bestowing life, creativity, and love. We will be using the term *yoni* to bring appreciation and acknowledgment—so often lacking in Western cultures—to the creative power this magical part of the female body holds.

Many psychological traumas are stored in the body and a large percentage of these are stored in the yoni. We are not only speaking of sexual trauma here. The yoni, as one of the most essential parts of our being, naturally stores emotional and energetic imprints we pick up in our lives. It makes sense to work with trauma directly at the source, in the body tissue where it's stored. Releasing the patterns of tension in the tissue can help release trauma and remove psychological blockages, which can be tremendously more effective than simply talking about them. This is why working with a crystal egg has the power to help you heal old wounds and awaken the life and love you truly desire. However, if you notice stirring emotions when you work with your egg, remember to be gentle with yourself. Go slow. Consider taking a break to journal, rest, or spend time in nature.

It's estimated that women have been practicing this ritual for energetic clearing with stone eggs for over five thousand years. Empresses and concubines of China's royal palaces used eggs carved out of jade to access sexual power, awaken sensuality, and maintain amazing health into their old age. Up until recently, this ancient, sacred practice was only available to members of the royal family and to a select number of Taoist practitioners. It was only when the first Westerner was initiated as a Taoist priest, around the 1970s, that the teachings became far more widespread in the West.

What Type of Yoni Egg Should I Use?

There are many kinds of crystal yoni eggs available. Below are some of the options, as well as the healing benefits they provide.

Rose Quartz

Rose quartz is the perfect crystal to start with and ideal for a sweet and gentle past lover. A partner that was good-hearted, kind to you, and caused no real trouble. This egg would soak up any last remnants and easefully erase any last threads of connection, in a sweet and compassionate way.

Red Carnelian, Red Jasper

This is the egg to use if the past lover had a very strong sexual hold over you. The red crystals hold a powerful Shakti, sexual vibrancy that will transmute your sexual attraction for them. The red egg will rest into the Shakti aroused place in your yoni and begin to settle down any excessive longing for him and return that passion back to yourself.

Black Obsidian

Use a black obsidian egg if your past partner was toxic, abusive, and damaging. This powerful egg will get to work immediately, cutting psychic cords, entanglements, contracts, violations of the mind, and any dark tendencies or strange holds over you. Black obsidian is *not* a good stone to start with. It is incredibly powerful and needs to be approached with utter respect and reverence.

Yoni Egg Practice Creates Positive Effects that Go Beyond Sexual Wellness

Inside the yoni, there are many reflexology points, just like the ones on the palms of our hands. They correspond with the internal organs—heart, liver, kidneys, spleen, etc. When you wear your egg you are massaging these reflexology points in a similar way to acupuncture, stimulating and rejuvenating the organs of your entire body. It has been noted that women who enjoy sex into old age tend to look younger and remain more vital.

Practicing with an egg increases blood flow to your pelvic organs and helps move stagnant energy. Stimulating the ovaries in this gentle way balances hormone levels and reduces PMS and menstrual cramps.

How Long Should I Wear the Yoni Egg?

It's understood that the crystalline intelligence of the egg will know exactly when to come out. But this kind of trust takes time and practice. You could begin by wearing it for the duration of the night. Then work up to wearing it for a whole day. Then, when you feel ready, place the egg inside and allow the duration to be decided upon by the crystal.

There are many different sizes of egg. For beginners, it's a good idea to opt for a larger one, as it's easier to wear. It feels more secure. As our muscles develop then we can choose a smaller one. In the beginning, the smaller ones tend to fall out unexpectedly, and if you're wearing it during the day this can be quite a surprise! Sneezing, laughing, or coughing can force it to pop out, so be ready to "hold it" with your muscles. Note: when using the toilet, be ready to catch the egg!

HEALING THE WOMB

Green Clay Ritual

This ritual is a deep and powerful process that should only be used when truly needed. This ritual was passed on to me a few years ago by a woman who gave birth to her stillborn child in a woodland near where I live. Days later she cried out in despair for help, and a way to heal and open to childbirth again. She was told to return to the place where she birthed her stillborn child and to bring with her some green clay and almond oil.

When this woman returned to that place, she was guided to create a small green clay phallus just large enough to fit inside of her, with a base that would connect to the ground at the spot where she gave birth. Once the phallus was shaped she left it in the sun to bake and harden. During that time, she slept, prayed, and cried as she remembered her ordeal days earlier.

When the phallus was ready she returned to the exact location on the earth that she had experienced this trauma, oiled her green clay mound, and inserted it in her yoni before sitting in meditation and prayer. She sat there cross-legged, with her skirt all around her. She realized the green clay was drawing all the trauma, sorrow, suffering, and debris from both her and her child into its constitution. The green clay was absorbing her pain. The location of her childbirth was supporting her process, and quite possibly the spirit of the child was also there, supporting, healing, and praying for his mother's release.

She sat there until she felt complete. Afterward, she walked to the edge of a lake and dropped her phallus into the water, knowing the entire structure would be dissolved and never re-form again.

As she shared this with me, tears streamed down my face. Powerful jolts of awareness pulsed through my body. I knew this was important, and that I had to remember it word for word. And I did.

Months later I found myself ready to experience this. This is a powerful clearing process for a woman. It clears the yoni, womb, emotions, mind, spine, and awareness of the female subtle anatomy. It surprised me how natural, comfortable, and healthy it felt. I have done this by myself and with a group of sisters. When with others it creates a spirit of togetherness and union. It brings joy, connection, and a sense of ease and naturalness. It is incredible and necessary for so many reasons.

Green clay is a compound of sixty to eighty pure trace minerals, fused together by heat in natural oxide forms and charged with an electromagnetic energy and a strong negative ionic charge. This gives the clay a vacuum-like ability to capture and discharge the positively charged viruses, bacteria, parasites, molds, yeasts, infections, and poisons from the body. I also believe it has the capacity to draw out negative traumatic emotions, thought forms, contracts, and karmas embedded within the womb. The practice of working with this healing clay ritual is a potent tool to clear energetic debris after leaving an abusive relationship and/or health-related gynecological disturbances and abnormalities.

How to Prepare for the Ritual

Green clay is a catalyst that supports healing without dangerous side effects by providing activation energy to the body. Clay has been used by indigenous tribes since before recorded history and by animals that go to natural clay deposits to self-medicate when sick or injured. Clay is described as being alive or as a living earth that can effect change through balancing, detoxifying, stimulating, alkalizing, and exchanging elements and energy.

This ritual involves making a green clay phallus that will be inserted into your yoni upon the land of a sacred site that is personal and special for you. As you sit cross-legged upon the earth, the clay phallus will draw toxins out from the yoni/womb and into the structure of the clay. The phallus needs to be small enough to be comfortable when sitting, and it needs to be shaped in such a way that does not cause discomfort.

After the meditative aspect of sitting in sacred space upon the earth—in prayer, intention, and breath—the green clay phallus would then be dispersed of, ideally in water. The green clay phallus will also be in union with the land, acting as a bridge between the worlds by bringing healing resources to you from Mother Earth, as well as the elementals of the sacred site you have chosen.

All of this can be discreetly done by wearing a long, wide skirt. When you sit down cross-legged, you can fold the skirt over your legs, and to the unknowing eye, you will simply look like you are meditating should anyone cross your path.

⚕The Green Clay Ritual

You will need some organic green clay, organic almond/coconut oil, and rose water.

1. Choose a day that has meaning for you. Perhaps this would be a new moon (inviting in) or a full moon (letting go). Become aware of everything involved as you prepare for this ritual—the setting as you mix the clay, the water you use (spring or mineral), the bowl you mix it in (please, not plastic), how you mix (ideally with your hands), where and how you bake the clay, and where you are going to sit on the phallus. Also, what will you be wearing, and how will you hold yourself, your composure, and your intention during this ritual?

2. Shape the clay to a comfortable fit. It's best to make a phallus of two to four inches in length. It's not about size here; it's about comfort with insertion. All you need is for the phallus to be inside the yoni, and for you to be able to sit on it comfortably. While shaping the clay, ask and pray for this phallus to be healing for you. Perhaps draw upon

the sacred masculine within the Green Man (the masculine aspect of nature) to imbue his healing properties into your work.

Make sure your phallus is on a green clay base so that it can rest upon the earth in a stable fashion. I suggest the base should be the size of a salad plate, not a dinner plate.

3. Bake the phallus. If you live in a hot environment, then leave it outside in the sun to harden. Otherwise, place it in the oven until hard.

4. Go to your sacred site with your oil. You'll need to lubricate the phallus with organic oil before you sit on it. Find your spot, settle yourself, and sit upon the phallus. Stay there for about thirty minutes or until you feel the ritual is complete. During this time, you will be praying for healing, purifying, releasing, good health, and being free of all cords, attachments, debris, karmas, and dis-eases.

5. Remove yourself from the phallus and bring it to some body of water. You may either stand at the side of the water or walk into it as you offer your phallus to the water element for dissolution. Know that when you drop the clay into the water it will completely dissolve leaving no trace of its existence. See all the debris contained within the phallus completely dissolving. Do *not* swim in the water where this is taking place. Leave the water alone to do its business.

Anoint the yoni with oil and rose water as a blessing and to rehydrate her.

It Is Done

Transmission

Kiss of the Crone*

And so here we are. Backed into that very same corner that Andrew squeezed me into at the white lion sanctuary. No more wiggle room and no more hopeless attempts to escape. Now we are going in to find that mystical part

---

*An audio track of this meditative exercise can be downloaded at audio.innertraditions .com/fiferi.

of us that can and will tell us, in no uncertain terms, what we are capable of in a time like this. We're going to meet the Crone. With great respect and pounding heart, let's walk into the dark embrace of a cave, to meet a fully palpable, utterly undeniable full-fledged Crone and receive her deep and penetrating kiss of gnosis.

She is there, hungry to transmit her Truth. Just like the Grail legends of the loathly lady—the Crone will always wish to get up close and personal. Only the innocent of heart can truly know her. It takes time to rid ourselves of conditioning and the aching chasm that separates the Crone from our beautiful acceptance.

The Crone brings otherworldly power, indifference to vanity, sacred rage, "I don't give a fuck-ness," and the key to womanly wildness. She knows what our capacities are and what we could become should we drop the fear of our own Light and power. She insists that we ask, "What more can I give? What is the next level of my contribution to this world?"

Come into a comfortable, lying-down position with your feet flopped open and your palms face up. Close your eyes and sink into the familiar presence that is your inner Self. Use your breath to drop, to dive, and to surrender. We're going on a journey to meet the Crone—a wild, fearless ancient feminine presence that will appear as yourself, and is yourself, but is also much, much more.

As you lie here, be brave and welcome this part toward you. You will need courage and vulnerability. Allow yourself to open to something unknown and something very confronting. With every breath, drop your shoulders and loosen your jaw as you find yourself walking, late at night, along the wild seafront of a mystical, secluded bay. It is dark, it is rainy, and it is cold. You wrap your coat and scarf around you tightly wondering why on earth you are being drawn by this desire to go and see that which is Her. You know that you have been summoned. You would much rather be at home in bed, tucked in and warm, and instead you are getting blown around and soaked by the ocean. The gray mist rolling off the ocean and the challenging confrontation of a storm meet you here. You know there is a cave in this cliff side—you've been aware of this your whole life. You used to play in the mouth of the cave when you were young, but you never went in too deep. You sensed there was something there watching you. It wasn't scary, and it wasn't friendly—it was simply a witnessing presence, and for some reason tonight you're being drawn to this very cave.

You see the cave up ahead, and there's a faint candlelight flickering all by itself in the entrance to the cave. One long candle stands there, right in the middle of the opening. She knows that you're on your way. There's a deep vibration coming from the cave, and yet it's not a sound, it's more of a presence. The whole cave is rumbling with this tone. You can even see the sand on the floor gently quivering. This tone causes you to become a little disoriented. As you step into the entryway, you start to feel a magnetic pull into the cave. This frequency, this vibration, is everywhere; it's outside of you, and it's inside of you.

Everything tones with Her presence. The storm, the ocean, and the wind are now so very far behind you. You loosen your coat and untie your scarf and drop them both to the floor. There's an inevitable surrender now; it's as if you are hypnotized. Gently drawn by invisible, ancient fingers. Every now and again, the odd candle lights the way into the cave's tunnel.

As you go deeper and deeper into the cave, everything external dissolves behind you. You are being summoned and you are absolutely at peace with this because it's time, because it's now, and because it's here. The deeper you go, the warmer it gets. There is something comforting about this warmth, and something quite nurturing about it. It is safe, and it is edgy. You hear movements in front of you, shuffling, clinks, clunks—maybe bowls, plates, cups. Someone is up ahead, and you can hear a shuffling of footsteps, the odd mumble, and an old whisper. There is a strong aroma toward the back of the cave that is pungent, old, familiar. It's not flowers; it's a musk. It could even be venom from a snake, a toad, or from a scorpion. As you lean into this smell you recognize it as an elixir—a highly crafted, skillfully made, powerfully present elixir. You can hear other creatures too. Maybe it's bats, maybe the odd cat, or maybe something else?

A bell sounds and the energy in the cave becomes crystal clear. Everything is incredibly silent. A form appears before you, dark and shrouded. Absolutely the same height and the same shape as you. You cannot see the face because the hood is drawn up. But you can see the bare feet and hands. She is standing right in front of you and breathing. You can hear and feel her breath. It's as if the whole cave is breathing with her. She takes a step closer as she reaches for the rim of her hood and draws it down to her shoulders. And you get to see who is in front of you—and it's yourself. A very, very old version of yourself. An elderly version of yourself. She stands there—unapologetically naked. Her cloak is tied at her neck and underneath she is bare skinned. She's not ashamed of what she looks like. You can see your own body that has aged and been weathered by human life. Her breasts completely sagging and hanging low. The lower abdomen rounded and drooped. The flesh over the knees drawn and crinkly. The skin on the neck sagging with age. The face weathered, wrinkly, leathery. Teeth missing, hairs under the armpits and on the legs, and a few on the face. Long, wild hair matted and tangled. And she just stands there—powerful, strong, and grounded.

This is what is waiting for you. Drink it in. Look at Her. Absorb Her. See, feel, hear, smell, taste—everything. You become Her and your positions are suddenly reversed. You look back at your younger self. Noticing all your ideas. The 101 thoughts going through your head as your mind tries to compute what you are seeing. Your heart beating with anxiety, fear, and interest. You see how you come and go, present one moment, lost the next. You sense your awkwardness at seeing your older self's wild nakedness, as you stand there, refusing to back down. You reach for your younger self's hand. It's sweaty, trembling. Your hand is bony, strong, gripping. You lead your younger self to a place where you can both sit together. You are the full and accumulated wisdom of this lifetime. You have seen it all, faced at all. Peered behind the veils of illusion. You are authoritative, fearless, direct. You have one foot in one world and one foot in the other. You have knowledge of all things. You can see all things. And here you are, sitting with a younger version of yourself. And this younger version is so full of so many ideas, so many notions, so many false dreams. And there is a sense of impatience—but she's here nevertheless and with you, and so you soften.

You need to reach your younger self, you need to shatter the falsities around her. The wishful thinking, the rose-tinted glasses, the reasons and justifications, the denials, the apathy, the laziness, the New Age-ness, the dolly daydreamer. You need to reach the blazing core of your younger self. And you know talking is not going to do it.

You gather within you everything that you have seen in the whole of this existence. You gather the absolute clarity for the reason of your birth that was inseminated into you before your incarnation. You gather everything she will need to remember, quickly. And everything she will need to come to fruition. You gather the sacred fires in your womb, the tender waters in your heart, and the glittering clarity of your mind, and the deep well of your Soul. And you simply become all of that. You are a raging inferno of transmission. And then you lean toward your younger self and with a summoning grip, you reach for her jaw and plant an intense kiss upon her mouth. You press into her lips, as you infuse her with your ancient radiance. You imbue her. You transmit pure awakening. Womb to womb, heart to heart, mind to mind.

Your perception shifts back to your younger self and find you don't know what to make of this—a powerful elderly version of yourself is kissing you deeply upon the mouth! You recognize the body as your own, you recognize the hands as your own, you recognize the face as your own. You even recognize the scent as your own. But this sudden intrusion, this boundary-breaking totally alarms you. Yet there is nothing, nothing you can do—it is happening. The Crone is strong and insistent and filled with urgency. You can feel Her rhythmic heart beating against your own breast. You can feel the fire in Her womb as she presses her abdomen toward yours. You can feel the pulse of Her yoni, next to yours. And you can feel the absolute impact of Her groundedness drawing you ever deeper into the experience. This is a fully radical Gnostic experience. There is no place and no space where She is not. She has crept underneath your radar and is obliterating you. You surrender. You simply allow it to happen.

You wake up on the floor of the cave. You hear the ocean again, gentle waves coming and going in the distance, bringing with them a sweet, summer breeze. Golden sunlight falls on your face. You're lying there, bathed in warmth and goodness and tasting the ocean on your lips. Sand is all over your face and body, and you recognize that something has happened to you, something has been taken away. Something that was burdening you, making you heavy. It's no longer with you. You feel reborn, tender, innocent. You feel wide open. Something good has happened and it lingers inside of you. There is no sign of the Crone—only sweetness, only peace. And yet, there is this vague impression of the intensity of that kiss. Your lips are a little bit bruised. You have no idea what happened, and yet you do. You have no clue what was said, yet you remember. There is no point speaking about this to anyone; it's not really for their ears. This is your gift. This is your sacred moment. As you get up and leave the cave, you know you're never going to return. What has happened has happened. The transmission given, the transmission received. Who you are now is the backwater of what is to come. You are the ripple of change that has already taken place. All you must do now is live it. It's too absolute, too strong, too imperative to be denied or delayed, or tampered with. All you must do is be. And with grace, you walk away from the cave.

Along the shore, the sea is now tranquil, luminous, gently imbued with the same energy that was in the cave. There is a sweet surrender in you. Nothing matters now, other than resting and allowing the deepening to come.

May the grace of wisdom be with you, always.

When it is time: What did She tell you? What did She show you?

Please, write it down now.

The "Promise" of Technology

In the not-too-distant future, there will be a microchip that we can place under our skin to keep us disease-free for the whole of our lives. We will still age and die, but not by disease and not by pain.

This microchip, which will be the size of a grain of rice, will be in constant communication with the internet, sending moment-by-moment information of our bodily health and inner conditions. Every organ will be tracked and maintained, and every fluid and secretion kept perfectly in balance. The moment something abnormal is detected, a download of frequency-based, preventive medicine will be issued straight from the web and directly into our body.*

Sounds great, doesn't it? Can you imagine how sellable this idea will be? Can you already foresee how many of us will be in the queue will-

---

*For more on this see Anne Trafton's "This Ingestible Microchip Could Help to Diagnose Disease" on the World Economic Forum website.

ingly offering our arm for the procedure? It's frightening and stranger than fiction, and yet we know, it is absolutely on the radar and already being tested out.

If we lived in a benevolent society where genuine health care was administered by natural, noninvasive, mind-body-soul-Light medicine, then perhaps this would be a grand idea. But we don't. We currently live in a society where God knows what might be going into our body—not to heal, but to control. The pharmaceutical industry is, well, let's just say *compromised*—we all know that. As for the internet? It's a neutral player—it will do and become anything according to its programmer. Placing these two organisms together in our current world is like offering our wrists and saying, "Take me now."

This, beloved friends, is our future. The promise of the fifth-generation (5G) wireless network brings us the technology to unlock doors, turn on lights, pay by swiping, and log into computers with a wave of the hand. What it doesn't promise us is the assured safety of humans and the environment, and this is even admitted by the industry. This unknown future of ours needs to be placed firmly in the hands of grace—and it is up to us to ensure that it is.

Pause here for reflection. Take the time that is needed to truly be with these insights and understandings. Just breathe and be with them. Let's bear witness to the sobriety of the situation and feel one another as we rise together to receive more of Her transmission.

Let's move on without answers.

We must learn to trust the process, remembering that *this is an initiation.*

Part Three

Permission and
Power to
Speak Up and
Speak Out

SEVEN
Accountability, Boundaries, and Integrity

THE NEED FOR A NEW PARADIGM cannot be fully recognized and accepted until the corruption of all aspects of the existing model are perceived and the true nature, extent, and consequences of the crisis are understood. And the only ones who can lift this veil will be the way-showers, pioneers, visionaries, speakers, and performers. In other words, the ones saying yes to this transformation.

It is up to us to step up to the stage and become visible. More than ever, it is our task to bravely imagine, decide upon, and speak out about what needs to be done—and then do it. So many of us imagine that we are already leaders, and that could be the problem. Our imaginings are not our happenings, and we need to create the bridge that links the inside to the outside, that births what we see into reality. We must be willing to endure what it takes and spend the time that it takes to get our creations off the ground to become a visible and powerful influence in the world.

Too many of us pull back too soon, instead of digging deeper into the ground of our being and taking on our becoming. Beyond the deceit of our fraudulent natures, the existence of a far greater inclination exists and is evident in our transcendental identity. The transmission of the Fierce Feminine is to urgently bring this down and into form. This covenant that we make with Her will birth within us the ability to transcend this fear-based paradigm and restore our resonance with the Light.

The most grounded and quick-to-experience changes that we can bring into our daily lives are boundaries, accountability, and integrity. Remember, She is attempting to overlay a template of becoming that is not only reachable for us but lasting. Her methodology is to place within our grasp a step-by-step blueprint that is implemented by vigilance and desire.

For this chapter, the keyword to recognize is *response*. She is inspiring us to respond, not react. She wants to place within our reach a catalyzing force of awake presence that does not look away, does not pretend it's not happening, and does not blame anyone else but shows up for life in the most appropriate and far-reaching ways. She is passing us the tools to be able to do this. For too long we have had our heads in the sand, being almost unaware of the bullshit all around us. We have given our power away to politicians, partners, and parents; and this has to stop. In a three-part wake-up call She clearly spells it out:

- First, discard what anyone else may think of us.
- Second, cease playing/paying for the popularity vote.
- Third, stop prostituting our creative visions into a watered-down betrayal of our early genius.

Her words are like a hard-hitting meteor bursting across our inner sky. She tells it like it is and implores for us to do the same. She challenges us to truly wake up and get up off our couches to become potent, provocative, and prophetic in our apocalyptic times. In our bellies there needs to be a fire, an inferno in fact, of raw, resounding passion that delights and thirsts for our waking up.

There was a time in my life when I was receiving a tremendous amount of flak for the things I had done in my past, and it came out in a public way (which is what happens when you're someone who is visible). There were a lot of rumors flying around, lots of gossip and lots of unwanted and unasked for opinions! So I decided to speak to everyone, publicly, all at the same time and simply declare the ground that I stood upon. I was not going to offer any excuses, reasons, or justifications for my behavior, just a statement of who I was in that moment. After that, it was pure silence. There was no more gossip, no more questions, and no more hassle. I had drawn a line in the sand, and no one dared cross it.

Below is the gist of what I stated:

This is my mark. This is what I stand for. This is what I am going to do and say, with or without your support. Yes, I have made mistakes, and I have learned from them. And it is because of this great learning that I am going out there, making sure my voice and the voices of others are heard and that action is taken. This is not a fame campaign. Or a marketing strategy. I am not here to be "liked." Or scorned. I have made major errors and with major errors comes major learning.

BOUNDARIES

Those of us with weakened or nonexistent boundaries are more prone to challenges from cult entity attacks/interference injecting through the cracks of our energy body due to lack of embodiment, or past wounding/trauma because we have not fully anchored our Soul essence into our body/avatar. I thought I was well-embodied until I realized how weak I became when challenged by others. I was afraid of how vast and lasting my power could be. But I'm not anymore . . .

I am witnessing so many beautiful, heartfelt women being initiated by the Fierce Feminine. It's not easy, that is true. It's not easy when you're so often led by a loving and welcoming heart to then reach for a different kind of love—the love of what's right and what's true—and to then rise as Her and express your no in such a way that your oppressor is made impotent. But it's not about a war, and it's not about a fight. It's not about arguing or mind games. It's about your no meaning no.

The Fierce Feminine is not obliged to recognize man-made law; only natural law gets Her attention. I believe we are to be like nature and do the right thing for the right people. Nature will look after her own.

Another area that may need our attention is the awareness of our red flags. Are we able to feel our internal warning system that goes off when something feels wrong? Sometimes it's a subtle feeling that something "isn't quite right"; other times we might have nightmares or daydreams and psychic warnings in the form of insights or visions. Red flags can also produce physical sensations such as restlessness, stomach cramps, jaw pain, toothaches, and headaches when the astral world is staging an attack. Some people feel an increase in anxiety or edginess, as they sniff out the artificial manipulation. But often, unfortunately, we say it's nothing. When, in fact, we are being bombarded with an astral agenda that is equipped to take on and take out our greatest intentions and creations. Be aware: all is often not what it seems.

So how do we strengthen our awareness of our red flags? By feeling for them, listening to their feedback, trusting what they show us, and acting on their behalf. Red flags are part of our intuition, a faculty that has been seriously compromised by our fast-paced, uber-productive society. Slow down, tune in, and believe the messages you are receiving. Trust them. Honor them. This conversation seems to continually come up, especially in our spiritual circles. How do we recognize otherworldly interference and the traps of agreements we may have made? It seems we are slowly coming out of a daze, as the veils of the false reality thin and lift. We are entering an age where we recognize that we need to be self-responsible without blaming. We must obtain our sovereignty on all levels and not follow or identify with any spiritual, religious, or political authority—savior, guru, president, etc.

We're beginning to realize the connection between psychological pathologies (such as narcissism and personality disorders) and the role of technology as gateways for otherworldly manipulation. We are understanding the necessity of embodiment, being grounded, connecting to one's own inner body intelligence and intuition, and steering clear of the trap of "living in the head."

Six Steps to Setting Boundaries in Relationships

These six steps were adapted from holistic psychotherapist Jennifer Twardowski's "6 Steps to Setting Boundaries in Relationships" post on the now-closed HuffPost Contributor platform.*

Step 1: Start with ourselves. We have to be aware of our feelings. To establish an effective boundary, we need to know what we feel and spend quality time listening to and honoring these feelings. Then we need to tune in even deeper to see whether our thoughts, feelings, and emotions are authentic, or whether we are playing an old story, or hiding from an invitation to grow. Discernment is the key, and this can only arrive with sincere and thorough contemplation.

When we do not honor our feelings, our boundaries will become wishy-washy and easily trodden over. This will lead to us to become entangled with the other in a messy and confusing way that often results in conflict and frustration. We must take the time to step back, tune in, find ourselves, and breathe deeply.

Step 2: Recognize how our boundaries have been crossed. We need to be able to see this clearly and calmly. Draw a graceful line in the sand and get specific. Invite our innermost self to reveal in what ways, how, and where our boundaries get broken. Allow ourselves to feel our response to this information before stepping forward proclaiming the valid need for a boundary. Make sure we feel safe before we move to step 3.

Step 3: Recognize the need to set a boundary. The next step is planning communication, getting clear on our needs and boundaries. This can often be the place we try to avoid because we fear conflict or defeat. So before we say anything, let's get clear and concise about what needs to be said. Remember, we are doing this as an act of self-love, and it is valid and necessary for us to feel safe.

---

*Adapted from Jennifer Twardowski, "6 Steps to Setting Boundaries in Relationships," December 7, 2017, *Life* (blog), Huffington Post (website) (although this platform is now closed, you can still read the post).

Step 4: Get grounded. Two things can often happen when we deliver our boundaries: (1) there's a backlash from the other person; and (2) we end up feeling guilty.

So now is the time to unite with our heart and honor our need for respect and acknowledgment. Engaging with the other's negative responses or arguments can often be a waste of time. Remember, our emotions are valid, and we are not wrong for setting a boundary. Breathe deep, trust the process, and know that it shall pass.

Step 5: Communicate! Take a deep breath and come forward. This is the testing ground. It's not easy, but it's vital that we do this. We are our protector, and so in that spirit, let's defend our beautiful heart and express with clarity our boundaries and the strength behind them.

At first it could appear that the other person isn't listening or respecting our boundary. That's okay, don't take it personally. Just be strong, reinforce your position, and if need be, be fierce! Make sure you are heard and walk away leaving the other to deal with his or her own feelings.

Step 6: Practice self-care. After exerting our boundaries, we may experience feelings of guilt and doubt that we did the right thing. Stay with the process and understand this can often be the lower nature playing catch up with our new growth. In times like this, we could go for a walk in nature or get some exercise. Don't spend too much energy focusing on what happened. Allow time and space to work its miracle. Stay awake! Remember everything that has already been discussed here in our time together. There is more out there than meets the eye. Who knows what the real agenda may be. So even if the other wants to talk about the "drama" of what happened, you don't have to go there. You can let them know you don't want to talk about it.

It's tough to take these actions. I myself was once terrible at establishing boundaries. I used to feel guilty or worry that I was being too heavy-handed. I wasn't, but it felt alien to me to be so different from the pleasing program. For generations the feminine has had no boundaries, She hasn't even had a voice, so this is bound to feel odd, uncomfortable, and challenging. But once you get the hang of it, you will see how it is the highest form of love and sets the container for a real and mature way of relating.

Men Can't Do It for Us

I'm noticing how men—and our own masculine energy—at this time can only support and cheer on the women (our feminine energy) in this time of great learning and letting go.

Boundaries, expression, integrity, and impeccability are up for women, as well as how to go about establishing these aspects in a way that doesn't get ignored. Now is not the time for the old masculine way of action only. The feminine is being asked to at least match or go beyond the firepower and magnitude of the masculine in the realm of boundaries and the expression of them. She must reach in and find the love, power, and respect for Herself—as Herself—and all She loves dearly. Then She must detach from the crippling effects of the female programming and take a strong stance on Her behalf.

Women, or the feminine part of ourselves, have been trained to be pleasing, polite, and agreeable and to not hurt anyone's feelings. We have been conditioned to not upset the status quo. And while there's a natural part of the feminine that *is* this way, it's only the correct path when it's completely authentic and appropriate. There is, as we are starting to realize, another part of the feminine that is discerning, that can cut through denial and illusion and is able to birth a new future for all. And it is this part that we need greatly at this time. The feminine must discover Her immense power to stand for truth, justice, and love as She guides humanity out of an unprecedented dark night of the soul. The masculine cannot do this for us.

So let us continue to see where we may still be hooking into the old paradigm and the belief that men—or the masculine—can save us. I believe that phrases like "Could you help me?" and "Could you speak to my brother, my ex, my father, my son, my male boss, the policeman, the government official, etc., and sort this out, man to man?" are of the old paradigm. I feel it is okay to ask for help, if we sincerely and absolutely need it, but help doesn't have to come from a man and the most valuable help comes from within. These are the "old ways," when it was good and noble for a man/the masculine to protect, challenge, intervene, and ward off. Now it seems all they can do is lovingly support and encourage our bold, brave words and actions of a ferociously feminine kind.

Our men want to help, they truly do, but I sense they do not know how. They feel a faithful reassurance that their beloved is working in the deepest and most incandescent ways for the furtherance of her Soul into form. And that is enough.

God knows I occasionally thirst for the old ways, where I don't have to face my challenges and monsters. Where my beloved would step in and make it all go away. But ladies, that doesn't make women of us— that merely keeps us operating as girls who are still asleep.

I believe this era is a rebirth for women and the authentic embodiment of the feminine into form. The Fierce Feminine is not only about being a lioness roaring to protect her cubs. There is another wilder quality that takes an even greater permission and a deeper surrender— and that is about burning alive in the fire of the Fierce Feminine and speaking with the voice of her pure lucid, lacerating, laser-clear flame of Truth.

ACCOUNTABILITY

As we rise and speak up and out, we shall become visible. When we are visible, we can be hurt. Visibility is an often run-from idea. One we shall have to overcome if we're choosing to wake up and respond fully to life or whatever is left of it. As leaders and wayshowers, we shall be seen to the very core. Most leaders worry about "losing face" or being judged. The truth is, if you lead, you have already lost face and are constantly being judged. So, in essence, it's going to happen. It's part of being visible.

When we are visible, we need to be accountable. A real leader is always accountable. When we make a mistake (not *if* we make one, but when—as it will happen) we are porous enough to see it, own it, and use our integrity to make sure it doesn't happen again. That, to me, is what makes a genuine leader and one we can safely follow. The problem is, once again, we have been conditioned to blame others when things go wrong. This, in combination with our entitlement, privilege, and often acute insecurities, feeds the forces whose job it is to make sure that there are no noble leaders, especially those who are cleanly and accountably helping massive amounts of individuals wake up. That's why it's imperative that we surrender to chivalric qualities of courage, honor, courtesy, justice, and the readiness to assist the weak and undefended. If there's a leader among us who is vulnerable, transparent, humble, and committed, then we stand a good chance of being invited to stay on this planet. But if our leaders continue to blame and shame, pass the buck, and conceal their true colors—then it's only going to get worse. The only place these leaders will take us is into the unfeeling arms of the death machine. A machine we've been part of for far too long.

To ensure that we're on the right path, and to minimize backlash, we can learn to ask important questions, regularly. It is through deep and honest questioning that aligned actions can be taken and our progression as a wayshower can become one of truth and vulnerability that imparts confidence.

The questions we need to ask ourselves are as follows:

- Am I living according to my values?
- Am I doing what I'm saying?
- What blessings have I been taking for granted?
- Have I allowed victim/entitlement thinking to creep into my life?
- Is there someone I need to forgive or apologize to?
- What relationship do I need to invest more fully in?
- Have I let anger of any kind take a foothold in my life?
- Is there a skill set I need to enhance?

- What project have I been procrastinating about?
- What excuses have I been making regarding nutrition and physical fitness?
- What problem(s) in my life do I need to take personal accountability for today?

The following are additional questions that are especially pertinent to this time we're living in:

- Am I taking more than I need?
- Am I overproducing, overtraveling, overspending?
- Am I a conscious consumer?
- Do I consciously release old items, or just throw things out?
- Am I giving back to nature?
- Am I leaving the world better off than when I first came to it?
- Am I freeing myself from every kind of negative influence?
- Am I choosing creation or destruction?

Our general reluctance to talk about difficult subjects combined with the ever-present excuse of busyness means that necessary conversations don't always happen and the consequences of this can be profoundly destructive. Hence these challenging questions must be asked often and regularly, and especially if something's troubling us. There's a Buddhist saying I like that illustrates my point here: "To catch the spark before it becomes a flame." To be accountable means to live visibly and with dignity. And when we live like this, the interfering influences that try to bring us down cannot touch us, as we are out of their grasp. We are free.

It takes courage to be accountable. We think of courage as translated into public acts of bravery by confronting opposing forces or challenging circumstances. But the linguistic origin of the word means "to take heart." Courage is the measure of our heartfelt participation with life, others, community, and work. To be courageous is to feel our feelings deeply in our body and in the world, to live up to and into the unending vulnerabilities of the relationships and aspects of this world that we care deeply about. To be courageous is to stay close to the way we were originally made.

The Fierce Feminine's transmission takes you to the frontier between deep internal experience and the revelations of the outer world. There's no going back once this frontier has been reached; a new territory is visible and what has been said cannot be unsaid. She wants to offer you a break for freedom. Every imagining is an emblem of courage and the attempt to say the unsayable, but only a few will be able to grasp something universal yet personal and distinct at the same time. Only a few will be able to create a door through which others can walk into what seemed previously to be unobtainable realms, in the passage of a few short lines and an unquestionable presence.

INTEGRITY

To have integrity means to be honest and carry strong moral principles. Many of us have elaborate yet small ways of looking like we're showing up, while not actually showing up. It seems as if we're there, but we're not really. And because of that, knowingly or unknowingly, we're blocking everything that's trying to come through our portal. This has tremendous consequences in our life and in the lives of others. The Fierce Feminine cannot tolerate this kind of foolishness—not now, not at this time. Having genuine integrity is a corrective to the doomsayers and donothings who are part of our problem. People who sit on the fence and play the "game" of waking up are dangerous to themselves and everyone around them. This is a deadly seduction of vanity and pride, and extremely stupid. We can all see when someone is not who they say they are. But now we must pay attention to it. We are in a time of chaos and change that is redirecting the compass of our contemporary culture. Ignore these words at your own peril. We must accept Her insistence to live with integrity. Not only will it help us humans regain our sanity, but it might just save our skins.

What Is the True Meaning of Integrity?

There are a few fables out there that can make us think we have integrity. Just because we tell the factual truth does not mean we are telling the truth! There are so many layers of intention, expectation, and feeling that must also come into view and be communicated. It's not merely about being honest or living a balanced life or even being consistent. It's more than that; it's an ever-growing and deepening way of life. It's not static. You don't ever "get" there. It's an evolving way of being, especially now in these formative times. I think I'm right in saying that we can feel when a person is in integrity. And I am pretty sure we can feel when we are in integrity. There is a yes-ness about it all. We make good decisions that are reflective of our values and beliefs, we are consistently authentic in every area of life, we are considerate of others and recognize the impact we have on them, and we are actively engaged in the development of our character and wholeness while enrolling others to be on the same journey.

Many of us say we *really* want this, but we're struggling all the same. And as we now know, there is a whole host of influential reasons ready to drop into our awareness and serve us in another direction. That is why a relationship based on these values is the fast track to integrity. If we can reflect back to the other the moments when their guard is down, in a way that the other can hear and not defend against, then we will be infiltrating the mechanism that infects and disables our natural inclination to become more whole and awake.

But we, as human beings, are quite extraordinary in that we can actually refuse to be ourselves. We can become afraid of the way we are. And we can temporarily put a mask over our face and pretend to be somebody or something else. And many of us can do that for the whole of our lives.

As Bernhard Guenther notes in his web post "Organic Portals: Soulless Human":

These are interesting times. On one hand, there are changes happening on a global scale that can't be ignored much longer. On the other hand, the majority of the population seems to live their lives as if everything is just as it always is and always will be, locked in a tunnel vision of personal and material interest.

As long as we keep lying to ourselves based on conditioning, wishful thinking, suppression or denial and believe the lies "out there" mistaking them for truth, nothing will change. This goes also beyond having a "positive" attitude, where hope can be merely a trap and lie to the self. Believing in lies that are "positive" in appearance (regardless of how well-meaning the intent or good-hearted the person) is actually being negative and blocks one's awareness and spiritual evolution. Being positive can mean acknowledging something is negative because it is the truth, seeing it for what it is. If you believe a lie, even if it seems positive and makes you "feel good," you give away your free will and that has spiritual implications. In these times of transition, it becomes imperative to seek truth and strive toward objectivity so we don't take the "wrong" turn into entropy.*

May every word above inspire you to keep on searching for truth and encourage those who are silent to step forward. Despite my best intentions, I realize that I have barely scratched the surface of what there is to reveal. There was simply not enough time or space within these pages. The search for truth and its exposure is of paramount importance. As time passes, it is slowly and deliberately being either entirely removed or more subtly eroded away. Without a doubt, truth is disappearing from our radar. Opposing forces present themselves continually and I suspect this will always be so. Take heart, be brave, and never be intimidated by anyone—ever.

---

*Bernhard Guenther, "Organic Portals: Soulless Humans," Veil of Reality (website), April 18, 2011.

Dairy Farming

Again the film *Land of Hope and Glory* is an excellent source for uncovering the truths behind the farming industry. Information about the horrors of dairy farming as shared in the film is provided below.

Cows are mammals who, like humans, only produce milk to feed their children. Therefore, for a cow to produce milk, she must first give birth to a calf. This means dairy cows are impregnated every year in order to keep a continuous milk supply. This is done through artificial insemination, a process in which semen is first obtained from a bull before being injected inside the uterus of the female dairy cow. The farmer does this by inserting his arm inside the cow's anus and holding her cervix in place before sliding a needle through the cervix and injecting the semen inside of her.

Calves would naturally feed from their mothers for around nine months to a year, but dairy calves are taken from their mothers normally within twenty-four to seventy-two hours of birth. This is done in order for the farmer to ensure as much milk as possible can be acquired from the mother. This is an incredibly traumatic experience for both mother and child and both will cry out for days.

If the calf is female she will be separated from her mother and kept in solitary confinement with barely any room to move. Legally she is only meant to be kept in these crates for eight weeks; however, it has been documented on UK farms that the calves are kept in confinement for as long as six months. She will then face the same fate as her mother: being forcibly impregnated continuously so her udders can be pumped for milk that will be consumed by humans.

The process of milking is grueling and relentless, as dairy cows have been modified to produce up to ten times more milk than they would naturally. This overmilking causes diseases and infections like mastitis, a bacterial infection of the udder, which affects around 30 percent of UK dairy cows.

After around four to six years, or when the cow is too weak to continue, she is sent to be slaughtered, even though a cow's natural life span is around twenty-five years. There is a misconception that buying dairy means that cows don't have to die, however all dairy cows are slaughtered, and each year around 150,000 cows are slaughtered while still pregnant.

If the calf is male, he will be of no use to the dairy industry and generally less suitable for beef production. This means that every year around 90,000 male dairy calves are shot soon after birth and discarded as a by-product. Male calves that are not shot will instead be raised for veal either in the UK or in Europe, meaning that the calves have to endure long traumatic journeys as they are either transported out of the country to their deaths or to slaughterhouses here in the UK. . . .

Dairy cows are often subjected to further abuse, with UK farmers documented kicking mother cows and beating and throwing newborn calves. . . .

In the UK we are led to believe that dairy and beef cattle are allowed to roam freely outside. However, in almost all cattle farms the cows are kept in housing for at least some part of the year and, in many cases, cows are raised in intensive farms where they are denied access to the outside for their entire lives.

When the cows have reached slaughter age, they are herded into trucks and trailers and are transported to their deaths. Once the cows arrive at the slaughterhouse they are individually forced into the stun box where they panic and fight for their lives. . . . It is estimated that between 5 to 10 percent of cattle are not stunned effectively and will have to endure the experience of being shot repeatedly in the head or having their throat cut and their blood drained while still fully conscious.*

Factory farming is where we find the most heinous acts of torture to the animals in our food chain. If you are a meat and dairy eater, please realize what you may be buying into. If you choose to continue eating meat and dairy, then please buy your products from small and local farms. I would even go so far as to say, visit the location, ask to see the conditions of the farm, and spend some time seeing where the animals graze and interact with one another. We have to stop being so disassociated from our food and its origins.

Pause here for reflection. Take the time that is needed to truly be with these insights and understandings. Just breathe and be with them. Let's bear witness to the sobriety of the situation and feel one another as we rise together to receive more of Her transmission.

Let's move on without answers.

We must learn to trust the process, remembering that *this is an initiation.*

Land of Hope and Glory, created by the founders of animal rights organization Surge with research and editing done by Ed Winters and Luna Woods, 2017, Land of Hope and Glory: UK Animal Farming website. You can find a full list of the public investigations featured in the film on the website as well as additional facts and references.

EIGHT
Sacred Rage

ACCEPTANCE IS unacceptable.

There is an aspect of the feminine that has—until recently—been heavily denied, frowned upon, and severely judged, and that is sacred rage. The reason this rage is called sacred is because of the nature of its expression. As we turn these pages, we are realizing how much we may have been in the dark (or not), and how there's so much happening on this Earth right now that's pushing the limits. The veils are being lifted, and the darkness is being seen. Consciousness is awakening and something primordial and wild is stirring within the feminine, as She fills with a rage that must be released.

Sacred rage is an explosion of wildfire that is both appropriate and timely. It's an in-your-face obliteration of everything that is untrue, unjust, and wrong on every level. It's not a personal form of anger; it's bigger than that. It comes in widescreen and technicolor as it galvanizes its power from the natural world and is often connected to the innocent and undefended. It's thunderous. It's free. And it is so desperately needed. Only the feminine within us can surrender to this innate quality. The masculine would never be prepared to be so wild and spontaneous. He values his quiet, calm demeanor. Whereas the feminine has access to this primeval instinct that is completely unreasonable and wildly powerful.

The problem for many of us women growing up is that we are conditioned to not be angry. From a young age, we are encouraged to be nice, pretty, agreeable, quiet, and smiley. Many of us were not taught the value of healthy anger, let alone the importance of sacred rage. We were not held or taught by the feminine to be *fully* feminine. And custodianship of the natural world is one of Her tasks and duties. If we, the feminine, do not and cannot protect the natural world, then I believe there simply won't be any resemblance of natural world left to protect.

There are times in life (like right now) when it's absolutely right to rage against the false and corrupt powers that continue to have influence over us. Throughout this book I have included thirteen "Sorrows of the World" that make my blood boil. What are yours? I believe it's critical that we ask this question. And even more important that we feel into our answers. It's so common for spiritual types to judge anger as a sign of being triggered. Anyone who expresses a strong response against something is seen as having an issue, probably from childhood, that needs healing. And so the spiritual elite develop the capacity to look on in serene passivity to every form of brutality and perversion as if their detachment was a holy indication of their impressive progression toward enlightenment. Little do they realize, their nonresponse is a by-product of their overmasculinized form of spirituality that renders them ungrounded, unfeeling, and disconnected.

Another great and well-trodden ploy by the false world of spirituality is to spin the yarn that everything is in perfect and holy order. I have been in communities like these—and they stink! Anyone who suggests there may be some imperfection is once again frowned upon and piously pitied for having an error in their perception. Such people are strongly encouraged to delve into their imperfect perception until they can see with the eyes of the enlightened mind and realize that the environmental issues that affect us all are not *real*. Yeah, *that's* a good one!

Juliet Carter, coauthor of *Worldbridger* and *The Template*, mandates sent by transcended beings, says,

Those who accuse you of being negative, see your ability to be "lucid without prejudice" as a direct insult to their belief systems; they make the mistake of thinking you are "against" something, when in fact the process of being "for" your truth creates the side effect of seeing the delusions that maintain the lies that stabilize this fear-based paradigm. They see the instinct to disengage from socialized spiritual circles as you separating from them, when actually you are simply unifying with your true self.

There is nothing elitist about awakening to what is happening on this planet. It does not create separation. It brings a more authentic connection to others through an expanded capacity for compassion as you gain an extensive knowledge of that which your fellow Humans are suffering through.*

This is a heads up with regards to the kind of resistance and judgment you may well come across, if you have not experienced it already. There is a growing group of people who are recognizing the infiltration of the New Age movement by a new spiritual "establishment" that have a manifesto of homogenized spiritual ethics that comes with a dangerous denial factor. Any discussion of pedophilia, genocide, and (in particular) the agenda of alien intervention are not welcome and can lead to not only being ostracized by them personally, but they may try to discredit you publicly on social media.

I believe the antidote to our paralysis is to first come into radical, humble relationship with the Dark Feminine, and invite Her to embody you. This is what I asked for, and this is what happened, and this is what continues to happen. For me, the Dark Feminine is the Black Madonna, or the Kali aspect of the Mother who gives rise to the voice and actions of the Fierce Feminine. The sacred rage of the Fierce Feminine burns through all the lies, illusions, and distortions. It cuts through to the white-hot truth. It's a catalyst for transformation and expedition. It births us into expansion.

Perhaps you are like I was, waiting for some kind of "permission" to speak up and speak out? Maybe you, too, are holding out for some kind of

---

*Juliet J. Carter, "Mindful Thoughts," Our Angels Guidance (website).

signal that says it's okay, you are allowed to open to this almighty and holy power? Well, allow me to be that voice of catalyzing permission. Let us take this forbidden journey to the pulsing center of our sovereign power.

For many of us, this has been taboo, a place to avoid or even deny. A place of fear shrouded in guilt and shame by the memory or projection around the abuse of that power. But now is not the time to buckle under the foreboding presence of possible past mistakes. Now we must access this vortex of both horizontal and vertical alignment and with great correctness say, "Yes, I am worthy to embody Her."

For too long we have tiptoed around, too polite or paralyzed by the opinions of others to step into this clean and articulate power that lies at the center of our womb. Its voice is the moral compass of what is right and what is wrong, as it considers all of life in its choices. Within our womb is a collective "No!" that is so far-reaching and unyielding that everything it turns its attention to will stop in an abrupt end. This power is our forbidden "truth bomb," a harbinger of justice and aligned ways and finally, today—may we not be afraid of it.

ACCESSING OUR SACRED RAGE

Not that long ago I went to visit an Irish seer, who warned me that it was important to access my sacred rage. This is a woman who lives close to me in the South of France, and someone I consider to be a trustworthy friend and gifted messenger. She could see some intense, dark turmoil in my womb and pointed to the fact that it would be healthy for me to release it sooner rather than later. She advised me to connect with Kali and to be brave enough and humble enough to ask Her to embody and sound this wrath out. In a roundabout way, she said it was time to burn through all the invisible conditioning that diluted my potency, truth, and indestructible power. She spoke of how I had been harmed in the most dangerous of ways, and that I had to rip through all the veils that kept me from being Kali. Her message unnerved me. I was afraid of Kali. She felt foreign to me. I had ideas that I might become evil or damaged if I embodied Her, and to be honest, I was afraid that I would go on a rampage and spiral out of control.

All of this was the bondage that kept me small and silent to the fury within that, unbeknownst to me, contained gifts for my Soul's journey. I knew I had to burn through all this garbage and get to the molten core of my true self-expression. I had to scorch the invisible ties and agreements I had made with the centuries of feminine programming that kept me quiet and passive. It was now my time to speak up and out in a way that the whole world could hear.

And so I asked Pete, my husband, to help me. I asked whether he would accompany me to a remote part of the forest and stand in as my surrogate adversary. He agreed, but it didn't work out too well. The first time I prepared to release my sacred rage, I rolled around laughing because I was so nervous and self-conscious. I felt ashamed of letting go. I thought he would judge me, or worse still, be afraid. It wasn't easy. My attempts to be angry felt fake and silly, so we went home in silence.

The second time I tried, I burst out crying. I felt so frustrated and helpless because I knew the power I wanted to tap into wasn't coming to the surface. I felt impotent and this angered me, but not enough to break through. So once again we returned home. Now, in hindsight, I can see how these failed attempts were like piling on wood for the bonfire, but I didn't know it at the time. I felt angry, frustrated, weak, and incapable. All of these emotions were soaking my inner world with a petrol that in the coming days would feed the inferno that was inevitably coming my way.

A week or so later, I found myself taking two of my girlfriends to an old Knights Templar castle in the area. They were seeking the inspiration of the chivalrous values of the warrior monks and their connection to the Black Madonna. Pete was with us as we climbed the narrow pathway that led to the ruined chapel of this once magnificent chateau. Somewhere in the back of my mind, I sensed a divine orchestration was underway. My friends began to ask probing questions about the person connected to my sacred rage. They proceeded to inform me of what this particular person was currently involved in, and the scandalous stories that continued to surround this one. Because of my earlier attempts to oust this wrath, it wasn't long before I felt myself starting to become animated. As we walked on, it suddenly dawned on me where we were and what this castle stood for. I remembered how it was the Knights Templar who were devoted to Mary Magdalene, and how they preserved Her honor by worshipping Her in the guise of the Black Madonna. This imagery stirred me. Here I was standing upon Templar ground, listening to the unsavory exploits of a person that so needed to be stopped at every level. Then I realized, the stage had been set. It was to be here, at the Templar Castle, that I would release my sacred rage, because not only did I have Pete at my side but the full strength and protection of the Knights Templar, who adored and upheld the Magdalene and everything She stood for.

So I stood upon that precipice, looking down into the valley toward a venue that I knew was housing that particular person and I prayed with a trembling heart to Kali to come through me. I confessed how afraid I was of Her power and how scared I was of becoming evil or tainted with Her bloodlust. Despite my fears, I humbly opened to Her, knowing in my heart of hearts that there was no other choice. My health depended upon this release, and I knew I could go no further on my own. My friends encircled me adding their presence and support to the prayer. Pete stood behind me making sure I felt his supportive presence at my back. It felt as if we were all bracing ourselves for something we had never encountered before, but which we were willing to be part of.

We stood there in the silence sensing that something was about to happen. I started to breathe deeply to reach the molten core of the festering outrage that stirred in my belly. The wind began to pick up as an otherworldly presence swirled all around us. Sounds began to escape my lips—grunts, groans, and words that I did not recognize. She was coming. I could feel something else starting to take over. Suddenly I knew to get down on all fours and put my back into it. Once down, I started to undulate my spine with tremendous gusto. It felt as if I was plugged into a universal power source that wanted to explode within me. This sudden eruption caused me to growl with a voice so deep and so raw that I hardly recognized it as my own. I was no longer human. I had broken free and was now reorganizing myself on the other side of the veil as a formless, wild volcano of "No!"

The sound of my voice thundered into the valley. I was blown away by how deep and loud it sounded. Often in the past when I was angry I would end up crying and lose the power of what I was saying. But not on this day. Today I had become the Fierce Feminine, and it was through Her grace that I could safely ignite in this way. Despite the intensity of the situation, I was strangely calm and serenely centered at the heart of the experience. It was clear that Kali had taken over. Her presence was clean, direct, and ferocious.

The content of my message was the earth-shattering outrage of how so many people had been and were continuing to be harmed by this person's actions. I sounded out the frustration and pain I carried every time I heard another story of deceit, manipulation, and lies. I roared for the ones who had been bullied, threatened, humiliated, and spiritually abused. I was not angry at him, but furious at his actions. I intended for my sound to stop him in every dimension throughout all space and time. My voice, Her voice would hold him accountable. And in that moment, that was precisely what was happening. It was as if I were privy to the gods and goddesses that ruled the worlds and what happens when a human being is summoned to answer for their actions.

There's another aspect that needs to be mentioned, as this for me, was the most important piece. In the midst of this outrage, I remember looking down and seeing the venue where I knew this particular person was staying. A wave of personal anger came into view and I found myself starting to formulate a sentence that was going to be absolutely directed toward this person and laced with venom and spite. Just as I was about to scream this curse out into the world, my mind became whitewashed with silent emptiness. The sentence and the intention were gone! Just like that—they disappeared. I didn't know what I was going to say, and still to this day, I can't remember. All I know is that it was going to be personal and carry some kind of dark omen.

That is when I knew that She had saved me from myself. Kali did not allow me to bend Her power or usurp it for my own personal gain. She held me within a true and noble Light, keeping my purity safe and untainted. Everything that I had feared about Her was completely unfounded. It was I who was more likely to stray toward the dark and unconscious impulses of the lower material realms. Kali swerved me at the last moment from saying something I knew one day I would regret. And that is why I can say with the utmost knowing—Kali is trustworthy. She is True.

I opened to Her full glory and I saw who She was and what She serves. Kali is the Dark Mother who is here to awaken her crazed and psychotic children, and She will use anything within Her power to transform us. She is simply saying, "Either learn what I am trying to teach you, either accept what I am trying to give you, either burn with my passion for justice and transformation—or die out."

In that staggering, humble moment of direct connection with Her, I bowed my head in knowing. I realized how this aspect of Her was the most important mystical gift that I had ever received. She had initiated me into the unshakeable realization of my own nothingness before Her. I am no longer afraid of Kali, or any aspect of the Dark Mother. I trust this energy completely. And this realization brings tremendous relief to my Soul.

EXPERIENCING SACRED RAGE
A Man's Perspective

This section was written by my husband, Pete Wilson, as a way of providing a partner's perspective on experiencing sacred rage from the outside looking in.

During Anaiya's first try at accessing her rage, there was a bit of fishing in the dark for what she needed me to do so she could conjure up her anger. I could see and feel how frustrating it was for her, as the whole thing seemed so out of context and awkward. Then, out of the blue, an unsuspecting stranger wandered through this remote part of the forest and swiftly put to an end any last remnants of courage she may have had.

The second time felt much better because I knew more of what she seemed to need from me. So I got into the role of being provocative, bullying—unexpectedly loud and verbally aggressive. I wanted to frighten her into action. But sadly, I was a little bit too convincing, and instead of getting angry, she got afraid and started to cry. And so it was clear that this wasn't it either.

However, the day we went to the Knights Templar castle was a whole different ball game. Right from the beginning, I could sense that something else was present. I could see the perfection of this coming together with her friends, the location, and her now near-perfect intention and desire to do this. It was great that she had the support of other women. For me this was about holding space, and other than making sure she didn't or couldn't injure herself, my only task was to simply and actively listen and witness.

Here are a few things I learned that might be helpful for anyone else going through a similar process with their partner:

- Find out what her specific triggers are, so you can be the most relevant for her in terms of speaking, attitude, body language, space invasion, etc. Does she need you to "receive," or do you need to be more proactive and say and do things to help her get to her sacred rage?
- Don't take it personally even if you seem to be the focus of the fury.
- Don't try to fix her; she's not broken!
- Don't try to be too casual.
- Don't try to make what you are doing as something just "for her"; it's for both of you.
- Don't make fun or joke, at least not initially.
- Do be supportive. Find out what she needs—water, quiet, drumming, smudging, etc.—and bring it to her.

Fierce Feminine vs. Angry Bitch

When Anaiya first started writing this book, I asked her a question that I figured was probably on the tip of every man's tongue: "What's the difference between the Fierce Feminine and an angry bitch?" The short answer? Intention! The Fierce Feminine doesn't have an axe to grind. She's simply stating the facts, however uncomfortable they may be for anybody, usually a man, who is not operating at their own highest truth for whatever topic is in the spotlight. An angry bitch, on the other hand, has some personal agenda running. It could be that she's angry, bitter, resentful, tired, a victim, etc. all of which may or may not be valid, but if any of those things are ruling her intention with whatever she's doing or saying, then she's also not coming from her highest truth.

How to Hold Space for the Fierce Feminine

The number one thing you need to do to hold space for the Fierce Feminine is *listen*. She's here for your good, even though she might be provoking you like holy hell. And she is, quite literally, holy hell to anybody's ego. How do you know if your ego is up and running? Well, there are a few giveaways that indicate you're trying to protect your false self and maintain an air of being right:

- You find yourself defending something.
- You withdraw into your man cave or into a sullen silence.
- You flare up in anger and attempt to turn it all back on Her (not such a good idea, especially if she is in genuine service to the Fierce Feminine!).

All these recognizable tactics are egoic. Listen to what she's saying because it's a signpost to where you need to pay attention to something in your life, and it's about time you did. If she asks you a question, try to answer truthfully. If you don't know, then say so. Or ask for some more time before the answer can be given. Suggest how long you need and come back to her without fail. Don't leave yourself open for her to ask for your answer. Be on it. You could answer something like, "I don't know right now, but I'd like to get back to you this evening when I've had some more time to think and feel into it, so that I can give you an answer we can both trust." If you can, and you mean it, thank her for being courageous enough to raise this important subject. Bonus points are always good, but more importantly, it will encourage your woman to dare to go there more often. If she's speaking the essence of the Fierce Feminine, you could hear uncomfortable truths about yourself, and how she believes you are ready to live beyond it.

How to Hold Space for the Angry Bitch

You need to listen to the angry bitch too. If her anger is triggered by the feeling that you don't listen, then your ability to listen and not react will change the dynamic. She will feel able to trust you more, and trust always brings connection. So try it: be really present, hold the space, and listen, truly listen. We are programmed to believe we have to say something back—we don't. Try it more often and you'll find the many explosions-waiting-to-happen will dissipate and dissolve. If she persists and it gets worse, ask her what she thinks you are thinking (see the previous section regarding an honest answer). If she continues on by getting louder, angrier, more spiteful etc., then as calmly as you can, invite her to come to her Higher Self or whatever she calls her truth. Try it a few times, perhaps varying the words but not your energy or tone. If she carries on, and you start to feel yourself wanting to give it back, or that your boundaries are being trampled upon, or that the situation is going nowhere, tell her calmly that if she persists in this way you will need to leave the room for your own good. If that doesn't cause her to cool down, then quietly and calmly leave the room, telling her you'd like to talk more about this subject when you are both calm and able to listen.

SACRED RAGE AS AN AWAKENER

I believe there is a holy awakening of the Fierce Feminine happening now on the Earth, with sacred rage as the catalyzing medicine. We are now in a time where only this kind of expression creates the change, expansion, and transformation that is needed should we be given another chance to stay on this planet.

Sacred rage is what will move us out of disillusionment and birth us into the new Earth that is already existing in the templates of time. It is an awakener. But first, we will have to be humble enough to allow it to pass through us. Personal anger and frustration are not powerful enough to shatter the falsities that surround us. We will have to hand over our agenda and surrender to Hers.

We must allow ourselves to feel that fire within us, as it is the antidote to every kind of weakness and suppression. It would be a lot healthier if more of us felt this sacred rage and permitted ourselves the opportunity to sound it. From my own direct experience, I can conclusively say this wild rage propelled me into sacred activism, to becoming a person who is not powerless or unaware. I now realize how powerful and effective I can be, and it doesn't make me feel superior; it simply makes me feel whole.

We are here to uphold, protect, and sanctify that which is pure, holy, true, and beautiful on this Earth. We can do this in two ways: light and loving or dark and fierce. Either way, we are free to choose.

Transmission
Kali—The Gift of Sacred Rage*

Come into a comfortable lying-down or seated position. Use this time to relax your body, open your heart, bring spaciousness to your mind, and transition

---

*An audio track of this meditative exercise can be downloaded at audio.innertraditions .com/fiferi.

your beingness from the external world to the internal realms. Take this time to ease into the body, to drop down into the familiar sense of yourself—the real you, the true you, the honest you. The one that you have been since you were a child, a teenager, a young person. The one that the world couldn't hope to change despite its multitude of attempts to fit you into a box, a role, or a shape that was simply too small, too constricted, too tight for not only who *you are but* what *you are.*

As you rest here, as the waves of the transmission build, give yourself permission over and over again to unify with the real you, your real feelings, what you stand for, what you represent, what you care about. Connect with the unmasked you, the out-of-the-box you—beyond your roles and duties as a partner, father, mother, daughter, son, wife, husband—you as you are . . . naked, raw, uncontrollable, wild, free, pure, and innocent.

I am going to tell you some real stories of real events and real people, as we start to connect with our sacred rage and the burning intensity of our holy humility to be with that rage, as it is. I'm hoping that the stories will touch the place where your sacred rage is lying in wait, to be roused and awakened.

One of my stories is about the time I went to a battery farm. I didn't know that was where I was. At the time, I was camping quite freely, quite innocently with a group of people in a yurt. One day I went walking over the meadow and through the woods. I could smell this horrendous stench; it was utterly disgusting. As I neared the top of the hill I saw this low, monstrous building made of concrete. It was huge, and it was just wrong. What was this hideous, artificial building doing in this natural environment?! It was like a prisoner-of-war camp, and it stank.

I asked my friend who lived in the yurt full-time, "What's that place over there?" And he said it was a battery farm for chickens. I hadn't even seen what was going on in that battery farm, but my beingness started to twist and turn and heat up and grow agitated. A great dread flooded my body, and I was beginning to snarl and growl. I remember my lips were twitching, and my teeth were already showing, and I said I wanted to go there, despite the stench, despite the utter disgust at how wrong that building appeared in the natural landscape. I needed to get close, and the closer I got, the wilder, more intense, more volatile

I became. There was not one chicken outside; they were all on the inside.

There were no windows, but there was a little gap in the sliding doors that enabled me to look in. The chickens were piled in cages on top of each other. I can't even tell you what was what, and who was who. They were crammed into that building, and they had nowhere to walk, nowhere to run, nowhere to move. Their box was just big enough for their body. And the fraction of the chickens I saw were revolting—they didn't have any feathers anymore. That was when I started to come to terms with the absolute wickedness of our species. And if you've lived at all, you know that's merely the tip of the iceberg. You know there's much, much more beyond that. So let that energy roam freely within you.

There is another story I have of an abattoir. A story of people working long hours in the abattoir for next to nothing. These people are not on the books; they are instead getting cash in hand. They're there trying to feed their families secretly. They're there because life has been harsh to them, and this is the only job they can find. They are shepherding cows into the abattoir. They are bringing the Friesian (Holstein) cows into line and getting them ready to be slaughtered. And in the heavy sickness of the abattoir, in the conditions, in the fear of the animals, and in the sound of the inhumane machines lies the absolute stench of death.

As that wickedness grows stronger and stronger, they bring the cows into this narrow corridor where they cannot move left or right, forward or backward—they are literally back-to-back. And the look in the cows' eyes sets off rampant, nauseating waves of fear that consume everyone in the process. And these humans, in their wickedness, decide to stab a cow. They begin to stab it as it's already in line to be slaughtered, as it's already being consumed by fear, intense fear that is infectious. Every cow in line is filled with that fear and begins to embody it. And the cow that is being stabbed cannot move, it cannot get out of the way, it cannot save itself. Everything about this situation is wrong. Everything about this situation is wrong, and the cow that got stabbed and will finally be slaughtered will one day be consumed by us.

This is our sacred rage, beloveds. This energy here. And as you tremble and shake and quiver and sweat, as your heart pounds alongside mine, this is our sacred rage.

I have one more story. It's about a friend of mine giving birth to her first baby. She is already in a volatile, aggressive, and violent relationship, and she's giving birth. She's in a hospital bed with her knees up, and she's giving birth to her first child. She's young. And she is afraid. Her partner is fighting with her right there in the hospital room. He is tormenting her and hurting her and trying to control her, humiliate her, and manipulate her. And he decides to end the relationship right there, right there in the middle of her labor pains, in the middle of giving birth to her first child, as her body reaches for unknown forces and unknown strength. Her partner ends the relationship there and walks out of the hospital room, quitting his role as partner, quitting his role as father before he's even become one. Can you imagine how that woman feels?

So beloved friends, feel these wicked sensations, these stories of our species, and I know that you know that there are so many more. Even as I write this there are genocides happening every day to animals and to humans—Standing Rock, Fukushima, Syria . . . Sacred rage is not our own personal rage. It's the wild, mad injustice that we feel when we hear these stories of our own wickedness. As you come into contact with your sacred rage, let us take a journey now to meet Kali Herself. Kali, who is the embodiment of this—a volatile, tumultuous turmoil and sacred rage and a force to will justice into being. Let us take this as it is. We don't even have to try and mop it up or cleanse it or purify it or bring it into alignment with our spiritual barometer. We just go to Her like this, as this, and as we meet Her, She is this. Whether it is Kali, the Black Madonna, the Fierce Feminine, we meet the Mother Goddess, the ultimate Divine authority of sacred rage because She is sacred rage. We don't have to clean up our face or align our intentions or tidy up this energy, because She is this energy. She welcomes us, as we are—heartbroken, raw, agitated, wrathful. And as we stand before Her, Her body amplifies our sensations. She sees us; we see Her. Nobody is tidying or minimizing or correcting or spiritualizing—anything. She opens Her embrace to us, and we connect with Her, we dock into Her, we succumb to Her. Human and Divine, Creation and Creator merge together as an all-consuming wrathful presence of sacred rage. We are not targeting anyone or anything; we are simply being in that raw and honest truth-telling.

The oceans around Fukushima are polluted, we do evil things to the animal kingdom, we are cruel and abusive to one another, we are raping the natural world, we are wiping out groups of indigenous people. We are trying to build a pipeline to pump oil through Standing Rock. Digging down into the sacred belly of land that matters deeply to the indigenous people, to pump more oil, while totally disregarding the sanctuary that this land is to our most precious people. The Mother sees this, and we see this. Sacred rage is allowed to breathe, swarm, and extend, and be. As we merge with the Black Madonna, with Kali, She channels our sacred rage through Her Divine heart, filtering it of any of our own personal maliciousness.

We can see quite clearly that the human race has an ungodly cruelty within its nature, and therefore She channels a beautiful, rightful feeling through Her Divine heart. And then She pours it back into us. Our sacred rage comes back into our being—clean, honest, raw—and with clear eyes we can administer our sacred rage directly and with great success. Because it's not blinding us; it's not distorting us like the eyes of a serpent. We can simply go out into the world, whether it's by ourselves or with our families or with any other group, anywhere, and with great clarity we can say, "No!"

Be awake, friends. Be awake. Be the eyes that can see, be the ears that can hear, and be the one that is responsive. Kali, the Black Madonna, is with us now, and She will correct Her creation, and this may or may not include us. Be with Her; be with that force. When you feel your sacred rage, you are feeling the belly of Kali. Allow Her to correct the world through you, as she does through me.

As the waves of the transmission continue to come from Kali, from this Black Madonna, straight to you, allow yourself to drift into sleep. Trust this process and trust where it takes you.

May the grace of the holy Sophia be with us, always.

Starving Polar Bears on an Iceless Land

On December 11, 2017, *National Geographic* published a video of a starving polar bear that was seen by millions online, all over the world.* Paul Nicklen and Cristina Mittermeier, two biologists turned photographers and cofounders of the conservation group SeaLegacy, filmed the emaciated polar bear struggling to move and desperately digging for food in a trash can on iceless land. As temperatures rise and sea ice melts, polar bears may lose access to the main staple of their diet—seals. Starving and running out of energy, they may be forced to wander into

---

*National Geographic, "Heart-Wrenching Video: Starving Polar Bear on Iceless Land," December 11, 2017, produced by Paul Nicklen and Cristina Mittermeier, YouTube video.

human settlements for any source of food. Interestingly, feeding polar bears is illegal. And so, without finding another source of food, polar bears like the one in this video will have only a few more hours to live.

Within days of the video's release, it appeared in my news feed on Facebook. Immediately, I heard and felt Her undeniable presence asking me to watch it and endure my natural reactions to such a video. Even now as I recall that moment, I feel the importance of what happened all over again.

I was staying in a log cabin for a month-long vision quest with my husband in a remote part of the French Pyrenees. We had no electricity and no running water and were living with limited, basic means. Pete was making food on a gas stove, and I had a candle burning to provide light while I wrote in my journal. I noticed that my phone had suddenly picked up a signal, so I started to scroll and within seconds I was face-to-face with this video.

I braced myself, knowing this was about to break my heart, and pressed play. I ask that we all do the same. Not because I want us to get upset and angry, but because this video can rip the cold layers of apathy, ignorance, and disconnection that not only numb and harden our hearts but severely diminish our ability to feel, love, and respond.

We must do it. We must settle down, take a breath, and be the polar bear's witness. It's going to be intense. It will send you over the edge, but it's an edge we have to go over, if we are to awaken to this time on Earth. Our species has lost touch with our relationship to nature, and especially with the animal kingdom. For those of us who can, we must take every opportunity to feel, witness, and react against this holocaust toward nature. SeaLegacy's mission is to create healthy and abundant oceans—for us and for the planet. Be part of the solution by visiting the SeaLegacy website.

When I returned to the video months later and read the comments made by viewers, I wondered what the worst part of all of it was. Was it watching the horrible distress of a starving and desperate polar bear—or realizing how unfeeling some of us have become?

Pause here for reflection. Take the time that is needed to truly be with these insights and understandings. Just breathe and be with them. Let's bear witness to the sobriety of the situation and feel one another as we rise together to receive more of Her transmission.

Let's move on without answers.

We must learn to trust the process, remembering that *this is an initiation.*

NINE
Discernment, Depth, and Awakening in Relationships

RELATIONSHIPS CAN BE THE CRUCIBLE of awakening or become the perfect breeding ground for lazy, half-hearted behavior where no one grows or rocks the boat. Worse still, relationships can be transformed into vehicles of regression that lead to our worst shadowy and immature states. Basically, it's up to us, in every moment, to ask ourselves, "What does this relationship serve?"

Relationships have always offered us a fast track to evolve, but now, at this moment, they take on a whole new level for those of us who are seeking truth to transcend the social deprogramming of the Dark Agenda.

Discernment and depth are the two most essential qualities for the awakening process to take shape and become real. It is in relationship that we begin to develop not only these innate abilities but also the ground upon which to practice them. Only a relationship with these kinds of qualities at the helm will be able to withstand the times that are to come, and as you can see and feel are already here. Discernment births sovereignty, while depth serves embodiment. Awakening is the breath-by-breath commitment to be conscious, responsive, and gracefully showing up in new and unexpected ways. For any kind of relationship to work, both parties will have to be aware and agree to attend to their personal and collective wounding. This will include being able to confront our shadows, being aware and parental to our childhood wounds, being mindful of our religious and cultural conditioning, and being able to own up to our unhealed gender distrusts. All these subjects will arise in the deeper connections with a significant other. One of these subjects alone is enough to rattle our nerves and start us heading for the door, but if we truly want out of the anti-awakening program, we must settle down and do this.

To enter the arena of these relationships we will need a few essential qualities. We will need to have developed our own feminine energy so as to receive our self-love and be able to apologize and forgive. We will also need to have developed our masculine energy enough for us to be able to administer and respect firm boundaries and manage reasonable self-control. And finally, we will need to have developed an intimate connection with our Soul, enough for us to be able to sustain aloneness and periods of solitude for reflection, discernment, and wise counsel.

The three abilities—discernment, depth, and awakening—are essential and are to be carefully considered before embarking on these kinds of relationships. However, should you already be in a sacred, committed relationship and wanting to progress, then perhaps you can look at these three qualities as a marker toward higher ground.

The myth of relationships is twofold: For the unconscious masculine, it's the search for varied sex. For the unconscious feminine, it's the search for true love and the happily ever after. Neither of these fantasy projections exist; they are simply designed to keep us busy, distracted, and entertained. These insidious, widely accepted alien-generated ideas have hoodwinked generations for centuries, in the East and the West. Yet we still continue to believe them, handing over our power to ideas that aren't even our own.

Instead, we need to stand back-to-back and be on guard against one another's foibles and weak points of entry. To stand united against the tide of psychic harassment and weakened determination. In union, we have another set of eyes, another set of ears, and a wider screen of consciousness to pick up on the hunch that all is not what it seems in the hyperdimensional reality that bombards our inner world. Instead of disagreeing with one another's concepts or seeing one another's point of view as a threat to our own, let's learn to embrace what the other brings, and add it to our own. Not in a paranoid conspiracy kind of way, but as awake, clear, and expanded consciousness.

Be turned around on the subjects of money, sexuality, power, intimacy, kindness, truth, intuition, and the cleanliness of your pure connection to Source. Clean up one another's act by being the eyes and ears of a true friend. If your partner feels threatened by this in a big way, then they don't really want out of the program. But if your partner trusts your observations, knowing that they could well be blindsided into believing that they always know best, then maybe you are both ready for more veils of reality to lift.

Of course, we will all be wondering whether we and/or our partner are being true to the shattering reality of the Fierce Feminine, or whether we have our own personal agenda running with a view to stay small and discriminating to the changes She is attempting to birth through us.

I've been in this situation a few times, when the pulverizing force known as the Fierce Feminine bellows for me to awaken in a flame of blazing fire. There are a few hallmarks that reveal whether it's actually Her or a shadow impersonation seeking separation and control. An individual impersonating this force will moan and mope, drain and dull the living daylights out of you. They're only interested in you serving them, whereas the Fierce Feminine appeals on behalf of the whole of life. She seeks *everything*. She wants the whole of you to meet the whole of Her, and She ain't holdin' nothin' back.

The Fierce Feminine is appalled at the way we belittle ourselves. She thirsts for us to rise up and to end the limitless ways we cheapen, compromise, dilute, and prostitute our creativity and life. She despises our tendency to hold on to our illusions and in frustration snatches them from our grasp and screws them into a ball. She sees the greatness in us and the potential. She sees the abundance in us and our lover of life.

Her fury at our numbness maddens Her the most. Her scream is so shrill and so clear in the face of our apathetic moaning that every glass in our cabinet of neat and ordered control shatters into a trillion pieces. Only when we're on our knees, hopelessly grasping at all that has been broken, do we see the many reflections of the face that She knows and loves the most.

"Get with me," she says, "and get wild."

We must be ready for this greater relationship with life. We must know where we're going, even if we can't verbalize it. We must have a deeper sense of our purpose and destiny, even if it is not fully defined yet. It must be real and strong for us. We must be willing not to give ourselves to other attractions or seductions, knowing wisely that there will be purposeful forces of anti-awakening attempting to swerve us off course.

The Fierce Feminine is the imperative force of awakening. Your heart and its nonverbal communication will reveal who it is that stands before you, whereas your head will only continue to confuse you more.

TWIN FLAMES

I would like to raise an issue that has been deeply personal to me—the subject of Twin Flames. This a difficult subject for me to write about, because it has been a subject I have spoken and written about at length in the past. But it is vitally important to bring up now.

Twin Flames are two beings that source from the same soul. The understanding is that once upon a time you separated into two individual bodies, and you now stand before one another with the urge to merge, but also the trauma of immense and intense separation. Many years ago, I thought I had met my Twin Flame. All the signs were there—past-life memories, telepathy, deep sexual union, emotional intensity, and various other kinds of unexpected energetic phenomena. We entered this wild and divinely chosen love affair at full pelt and before we knew it, we were married in a little over six months. I myself had never experienced anything like it before in my life and haven't again since. And neither would I want to, and neither do I need to.

I have been looking at Eve Lorgen's work on the "alien love bite." She specializes in anomalous trauma, which is defined as "traumatic events that exist out of the normal range of human experience." These experiences may include alien abductions, near-death experiences, shamanic initiations, military abductions, mind control, spiritual warfare, demonic and psychic attacks, cult involvement, and narcissistic abuse.

It feels close to what I experienced, but I would like to add more here. I feel there could well be an influence that controls and orchestrates these false Twin Flame encounters. I know for sure my encounter was orchestrated from the deep recesses of my own mind. Earlier in this book, we covered the story of Bluebeard and how to survive the Soul's predator. Well, I know for a fact it was that predatory force that manifested itself as my partner all those years ago. No one can move me from that truth.

I can also see, in hindsight, that the predatory force, as frightening and as undying as it was, has now become my greatest ally and shadow agent in the invisible realm. I am not entirely convinced this is an alien; rather more of a fallen angel.

The reason I use the words *fallen angel* is because I could see clearly on the inside, and when manifest on the outside, this force wanted desperately to be not only good but Divine. I could sense that its capacity to be angelic was easily within reach, but just at the last moment it would swerve and be furious at its closeness to goodness and God. It seemed to detest close connection and despise love, yet, at the same time, be irresistibly drawn toward it. I often wonder whether these mistaken Twin Flames are conjured up from the deepest shadows within ourselves to eventually make whole and unified a being who was once so terribly fractured and torn.

Now, later in life, where I find myself again in a deep and growth-oriented relationship, I can see and appreciate the slow and trustable movement from one stage to the next. If you have ever been burned by a false Twin Flame encounter, you will know that it takes time and deep inner work to be able to trust as deeply again. But trust again we must.

I realize now, it was presumptuous of me to imagine I'd met my Twin Flame so soon after putting out a prayer. My level of beingness was joyful, relaxed, and open, but my mind contained some intensely dark shadows. That playful state could have easily been mistaken for Soul embodiment, but it wasn't. It felt more as if the playfulness were the outer edges of the Soul's radiance, whereas the presence of Soul feels deep, wise, and steady.

The hostile powers working against the embodiment of the Soul are always difficult to conquer. Ordinarily, we are in complete darkness or ignorance of the Soul with only flashes of knowledge every now and again. I suspect even when we have risen into the continual glow of knowledge and can discern the play of all the dark forces, we are not exempt from attack. Perhaps it is only when we grow serene through persistent and moment-by-moment full illumination that we are beyond their influence and energetically out of reach.

It is not only the dark forces who obstruct and make it impossible for the Twin Flames to meet, for even when they actually do meet their lives may become wrecked due to mental and emotional impediments. It is only when the Soul embodiment is predominant in both that the two can truly fulfill one another and progress higher. And as we know, it's rare but not altogether impossible that what God has put together must not be torn asunder.

DISCERNMENT

The subject of Twin Flames leads us perfectly into the realm of discernment in relationships. I am now in a place in my life where the suggestion of a past-life connection or the idea that I am part of someone's Soul family or part of a group of reincarnated Souls has zero impact on me. Even if I was to sense a glimmer of truth in what they were saying or what I was feeling, I would still proceed cautiously, making sure everything was filtered through my intuition and gut instincts. I am not enamored of these things anymore, and I certainly don't need to feel I belong to anyone or any group.

It is here, in this chapter, that I am going to share my most controversial and true-for-me contemplations. What I am about to share has been with me since I was a child. As I have matured, it has proven itself to be true.

In the Gnostic tradition, it's understood that there are three types of human beings. One type is purely of the spirit, a second type is open to receiving the spirit, and a third type is opposed to the spirit. If this is true, then some Gnostic researchers say that one-third of the human race is of the original spiritual race, while two-thirds make up the remainder. To me, this makes complete intellectual and felt sense. To be honest, it's completely obvious.

Let's take it a step further. The Gnostics inform us that the spirit of gnosis is contained within the blood, bone marrow, and genetics. If an individual is of the spiritual race, it will be true to say they have certain "supernatural gifts" and abilities that get passed on through their bloodline, and it will be strongest in the mother-daughter connection. The bloodline lineage I am speaking of is a maternal bloodline that began with the appearance of Eve.

It is my intuition that those (mostly) women are relentlessly hunted down by the Dark Agenda and its human and nonhuman offspring. And they have been for centuries. Within their blood is the "Starfire"— the frequency that contains the indwelling spirit.

Which brings me full circle. The Dark Agenda as we know it is indeed interested in maintaining control amid the lavish production of their resources, but I can't help feeling there is an added and urgent interest in these Starfire women. Speaking to those of you who know in your heavy and responsible heart that you are of Starfire descent: you have even more reason to be discerning.

For those who are not sure or have no interest in this subject at all, let's proceed with the more everyday situations and reasons that call for heightened discernment and awareness.

I have noticed, throughout the world with all kinds of people, that if you mention the possibility of psychic attack and otherworldly forces playing an active influential role in disturbing the growth surges in relationships, they all nod their head in agreement. Even my mother, who could be classified as "normal" and living a "regular" life in the British Isles, feels something like this could indeed be true. And yet our modern therapists and spiritual teachers will roll their eyes and come back to us with a classical spiritual bypass along the lines of "So what role are you playing in order to attract this?"

Great question, but not needed at this stage of the game. First, I believe we need to know, I mean really know in the marrow of our bones, that anyone who tries to awaken from the hypnotic state of human slumber will be met with resistance and attack, which can come through our own minds or be working through the people close to us. The tactics used include draining us, distracting us, and sabotaging any of our attempts to wake up and break free from the slumber. All forms of escaping the Dark Agenda are seen and responded to. That is why I strongly include discernment in the realm of relating. With deep humility, it would be wise not to assume we are immune to these influences. They can come through us, just as easily as they come through the other.

We must develop our own introspective lens and subtle detector of otherworldly manipulators and agents of disorder. Sometimes they work to keep us malleable and controlled. Other times they actively instigate rage, jealousy, and victim mentality to feed off our intense emotions. I have also noticed that there is a heightened chance of interference should there recently have been a surge of awakening and expansion into true beingness.

DEPTH

Depth . . . real depth.

To go to that place where we barely recognize ourselves and to commune there. That is depth. And yet there are few people in the world who really understand us—our true nature and the qualities that even we have not discovered—yet, anyway. At the surface of our personality, we might find much agreement but at a deeper level beneath our minds, there is a whole other realm that is filled with essence. How often do we go there with another, or even ourselves? To meld with another is to share our essence, and that is so unfortunately rare.

It's not about friends or popularity. It's not about talking endlessly or understanding one another's point of view. It's about feeling the ripples of our beingness and attuning to direct connection. To win favor among many people is to accommodate ourselves to their expectations, and this will weaken and even destroy our ability to recognize ourselves. People want to be loved, accepted, and acknowledged, and this is certainly driven by insecurity.

At a deeper level, we need a more profound recognition. We need a true ally, not merely a friend. We need someone who recognizes our true nature and responds to this naturally. We do not have to perform for these people. But we do have to honor this nature within ourselves. If it is unknown to us, or if we are resisting it or denying it by trying to be something else that we think will be more successful, then our relationship with these rare individuals will not come to pass, and we will have lost a great opportunity.

As we begin to go deeper and receive heartfelt wisdom, our criteria for relationships will change. We will seek presence and honesty. We will look for aligned values. We will look for steadier beingness and accountability. We will look for greater integrity within people, greater sincerity, more substance, and less fickleness and fakery. Make a note here—as these qualities will be looking for us too. Beauty alone will not sustain us. Wealth, power, fame, or sexual allure are not the qualities that permanently interest us anymore. Of course, this will rule out many people, as the deep-rooted connection will not be there. They are living at the surface, whereas we have gone beneath.

We cannot wait for them or try to educate or enlighten them, for this will not be productive. We must seek people who are ready, willing, and able to connect with us at this deeper level. If we try to inspire or uplift someone or bring them to this greater state of recognition, we will be wasting our time, which is precious.

Placing our emphasis on beauty and charisma is clearly superficial but so is placing all our emphasis on intellectual brilliance, status, and financial power. We are now listening for something greater and truer in ourselves, and that is why we are listening for the same in someone else. And it's not about words or inspiring conversations. You may talk about spirituality, you may talk about God, you may talk about awakening, but that does not mean there is a deeper connection at all.

You know what I mean, I know you do. So, please, trust your nonverbal inner guidance.

Taking this journey into the deep creates a wave of growth and awakening in every direction. As we slow down and become present to subtext and the ever-changing tides of our inner world, then so too do we develop the wisdom to be able to tune in to others in this same way. This greater capacity to perceive with the inner eyes and ears begins to open us to gnosis. Once this starts happening, there will be no turning back. The world of relationships as we once knew it bleeds into insignificance, as the real presence of love not only begins to take over but transforms us into a totally and wholly new caliber of being.

Now that we have developed the navigation and ability to tune in to this deeper and truer source of wisdom, we remember to take our decision-making and direction-taking to this still and inner place. If wisdom does not choose, we do not need to choose. If wisdom is not saying yes, then we do not say yes. If wisdom is silent, then we are silent. If wisdom is not committing itself, we do not commit ourselves. If it is not a yes, it is a no. There are no maybes.

In our deep togetherness with self and the other, perhaps we may get to realize there is a greater destiny waiting for us in the world. And we must say yes to this. There are others who are part of this destiny and who will play a significant role in its discovery and expression. We have a greater destiny and a greater purpose. We must follow this pathway and not give it up for love or money, not for beauty, wealth, or charm. If we do this, if we align with our true Soul's calling, we will become strong and mature enough to engage with certain people with whom we share this greater destiny. We will find them, and they will find us. And we will be ready for one another.

AWAKENING

And so now, finally, we come to the section of this chapter where we can relax a little bit and learn the extraordinary importance of being able to settle into our bodies. It is here that we come face-to-face with how essential it is for us to regularly bring in sacred touch, bodywork, breathwork, movement, and prayer to the body. This section is called awakening because I believe it is these kinds of embodied skills and practices that are the antidote to all the artificial shape-shifting influences that surround us. If you think about it, it makes perfect sense that the key to sidestepping this artificial intelligence is to be natural. Now more than ever we must remember the importance of relaxation, joy, laughter, playfulness, spontaneity, peace, comfort, connection, and all the wonderful forms of bodywork that are out there. We shouldn't resort to these practices only in times of pain or injury; instead, we should consider weaving them into our weekly, if not daily, lives.

There are a couple of practices that stand out for me, and are part of my daily life, and they are featured below.

Somatic Movement

The first practice I would like to highlight is somatic movement. A somatic movement, generally speaking, is one that is performed consciously with the intention of focusing on the internal experience of the movement rather than the external. I recently created a body of work called Sacred Body Awakening, and I was lucky enough to have a somatic bodyworker on one of these retreats. After I had demonstrated one of the first stages of the practice, she informed me that what I was doing was prenatal body movements. She explained how the rhythm and tonality in which I demonstrated the practice, and upon which I placed great emphasis, was the same rhythmic resonance as somatic bodywork. It was precisely these movements that unwind any kind of infantile trauma that may have been experienced in the womb and birthing process. It's this kind of touch and movement that heals at such a profound level, quite possibly all the way back to preverbal consciousness.

This touched me greatly because I knew within that this kind of touch, rhythm, and resonance was what the world truly needed. I believe it would be such a gift if we were to bring this kind of togetherness into our relationships. It would save us from overthinking and overtalking about our sadness, fears, and feelings of isolation and misunderstandings. This kind of touch effortlessly takes care of all the energetic debris that often clogs up our relationships. It is so relaxing, it is so obviously of the heart, that it brings about that deep level of connection that we spoke about previously in this chapter. I honestly believe that this somatic touch has the power to heal depression, lift chronic fatigue, and cure cancer.

Sexual Healing

The other modality I would like to share with you is the importance of being able to open, irrigate, and harmonize the tissues and cellular memory stored in our sexual organs. Embedded and encoded within our sexual organs, in both man and woman, are the sexual trespasses, projections, judgments, and shames that have come our way—either by one of our partners or from our own minds. Sexual healing is a beautiful, sacred, and mature practice of being able to help one another open and soften in these places. This can be done by consciously and heartfully pressing into the yoni, external womb, groin, and inner thighs. For a man, this would be the lingam (Sanskrit for penis), scrotum, perineum, and groin. For a woman, this can be done with the softness of your fingers (no sharp fingernails) or, when you are ready, with an erect lingam. Slowly and softly build pressure, using your intuition to feel into whether the pressure should be still or rotational. Ask your partner what feels best. As you begin to press into and knead the tissues around the sexual organs, ask your partner to tune in to the connection via your touch. Guide them to breathe deeply and inform you of any thoughts, feelings, visions, or sensations. It is highly likely that important material will come up from this healing touch. Encourage your partner to allow their emotions and to gently release any sense of trespass or trauma. It is wise not to analyze or talk after such a session, rather allow your partner to cuddle up to you or be left alone to process quietly and safely.

This work is just as important for the male, especially around such events as circumcision, penile size comparison, or any form of inappropriate sexual touch or trauma. Just like for women, sexual shame, guilt, and fractured parts of the self can reside in a man's genitals. These hurt pieces affect the other aspects of our lives, such as creativity, financial stability, steady sense of mind, robust health, confidence, and nonaddictive personalities.

Prayer

I would like to speak to you now about the importance of prayer. When I say prayer I mean an earnest, heartfelt, vulnerable, spoken out or spoken in intimate communication with God, our true Creator. It must be simple, and it must be real. Any kind of important hat or mask that we may be wearing on the outside needs to come off for this level of prayer work. This is a real and honest correspondence between that which has been created and that which is the Creator. There needs to be a reality check on how astonishingly insignificant yet innately important we are. There needs to be a sense that we are speaking to and with a mysterious force that is both mother and father. That is both light and dark. And when I say dark, I mean unknown. As the humility starts to come, that is the time to begin engaging in prayer. When I pray I send my communication out, and then I wait, listen, and receive sensations, knowings, and a sense of connection. It's in that connection that the insights and answers are revealed. Once again, through the body, not the mind.

The most astonishing levels of awakening have come to me because of discernment, depth, and awakening. I have become so remarkably close to others, myself, and God by these practices. And that brings me remarkable comfort. My last word on this is—do not forget about the body. The body is key to this new level of awakening. Flush the body of all trauma and disembodiment, and a whole new world will be revealed.

Nuclear Weapons

It was Ernest Rutherford who first conducted research that led to the splitting of the atom in 1917. However, it wasn't until 1939, when the first uranium atom was split, that nuclear power was discovered. There are now eight countries who have publicly declared their possession of working nuclear weapons. The SIPRI notes that "At the start of 2018 nine states—the United States, Russia, the United Kingdom, France, China, India, Pakistan, Israel and [North Korea]—possessed approximately 14,465 nuclear weapons, of which 3,750 were deployed with operational forces."*

---

*Stockholm International Peace Research Institute, "World Nuclear Forces," *SIPRI Yearbook 2018: Armaments, Disarmament and International Security,* August 22, 2018.

Most of the planet's inhabitants, even those who are highly educated and working in governments and organizations like the United Nations, have little awareness of what an exchange of nuclear weapons would be like or what its immediate and long-term effects would be in terms of the massive numbers of civilian deaths and the rapid deterioration of the planetary environment.

Since 1939, America—the first country to manufacture nuclear weapons and the only one to have used them—and Russia have been engaged in an arms race that has led, step-by-step, to the growth of nuclear weapons around the world, the greater part of which are situated within these two countries. The United States has produced more than 70,000 nuclear warheads, more than all other nuclear weapon states combined.* The launch of one of these weapons in error is a consistent possibility and would precipitate a genocidal catastrophe.

In a YouTube video, Anne Baring, author of *The Dream of the Cosmos: A Quest for the Soul,* notes:

> From a Jungian perspective, the whole history of the splitting of the atom and the development of nuclear weapons is a dangerous and unrecognized pathology, born of the cultural conditioning that men have undergone for millennia, and is based on rivalry and fear. It's very difficult to break out of this conditioning and to recognize the full horror of what they have brought into being and the catastrophe that could be unleashed on the earth and its inhabitants. It's also difficult for women not to fall under the spell of the belief that they are protected by these weapons and by the men who are controlling and developing them. In the words of Robert Green, a former Commander in the Ministry of Defense at the time of the Falklands War, "Nuclear deterrence is no more than a repulsive, unlawful pro-

---

*Christopher E. Paine, Thomas B. Cochran, and Robert S. Norris, "The Arsenals of the Nuclear Weapons Powers: An Overview," *Natural Resources Defense Council,* January 4, 1996.

tection racket used as a counterfeit currency of power but hugely profitable for the corporate arms industry."*

I grew up with the threat of nuclear war. It was a real threat in the 1980s; so much so that one day my father sat me down to watch *The Day After*, an American television movie that first aired on November 20, 1983. It was a rudimentary exposé of what nuclear war could be like. I remember my father making me watch it and then discussing it with me afterward. He told me that if I heard a nuclear warning that I would have a twenty-minute window to decide what I wanted to do. He said there were only two choices: one was to survive and the other to die. He said if I wanted to survive I would have to go underground and prevent myself from getting infected from the radioactive fallout. And that it would probably be a few months before I could tentatively venture to the surface of the Earth again, knowing that the water and soil would be infected. He said I would eventually find others, and that perhaps humanity would start again, but that the majority of our species would be gone.

If, however, I chose to die he told me to head for an open space like a field or a park and wait for the flash of light to completely disintegrate me right there on the spot. He said I would feel no pain, that it would be instant. He told me that he and my mum would choose to die and that I shouldn't use my twenty minutes to go looking for them but to be brave enough to make my decision and stick with it.

I'm not sure if any of you growing up in the 1980s had a similar conversation, but for me the threat of nuclear war was always close and increasingly real. I don't know whether it's because I had that conversation with my father or whether I, in my own right, was already attuned to this reality, but for as long as I can remember I have regularly had apocalyptic dreams. These dreams were and are so lucid that I can

---

*Anne Baring, "Anne Baring on the Splitting of the Atom and the Shunning of the Feminine," December 22, 2017, produced by TalkWorks Films, YouTube video.

actually read the descriptive code of each bomb as it descends to earth. Unfortunately, they always read "United States of America."

And so, for me, nuclear war isn't so far-fetched. I realize that it could come to us at any time and if that should happen, the world would be rocked by its effects. Even during the writing of this paragraph, I switched over to YouTube to watch the nuclear scene in the series I mentioned earlier and found myself crying and shaking at the unprecedented level of carnage and destructive power unleashed upon the Earth. We need to know the facts about why both nuclear weapons and nuclear reactors are such a danger to the planet, and why it's necessary for the feminine principle to raise Her voice against these monstrous creations of the human imagination. If we knew, or rather, if we could *feel,* what this would do, we would be outraged that the life of the planet could be threatened by our creations. And that much of its life and millions of its people would be extinguished by an exchange of weapons and the nuclear winter that would follow.

Pause here for reflection. Take the time that is needed to truly be with these insights and understandings. Just breathe and be with them. Let's bear witness to the sobriety of the situation and feel one another as we rise together to receive more of Her transmission.

Let's move on without answers.

We must learn to trust the process, remembering that *this is an initiation.*

Part Four

Piercing
the Veils of
Reality

TEN
Narcissists, Psychopaths, and Sociopaths

BELOVED FRIENDS, HAVE YOU NOTICED there's been an increase in narcissism and how this increase tends to mirror the explosion of the technological age? I am seriously wondering if the two could possibly go hand in hand. Is this fixation with the online world numbing our empathy and intimacy centers and diminishing our once-natural impulse to be with real people in real time? Are we changing the environment where we live from the physical, natural world to an online artificial one where real human connection, touch, and sharing are a things of the past?

Are we becoming hybrids—part human, part IT? Is this true evolution, or another invention of the Dark Agenda? It is a well-known study that teenage boys and girls prefer online pornographic sex than the real thing. Young adults report feeling awkward with others, unequipped and unable to communicate and stay interested, let alone have the desire to create and sustain intimacy.

Recent studies reveal the medical system still cannot accurately pinpoint what causes narcissism or how to treat it. The latest idea that physical touch could heal or balance psychopathic tendencies did not work. And so the medical/psychology industry is still at a loss, not knowing how or why this phenomenon is here, and why it's rapidly increasing.

A general understanding is that narcissism can be caused by mismatches in parent-child relationships with either excessive adoration or excessive criticism that is poorly attuned to the child's experience. Or it exists within the DNA and genetics as inherited characteristics. This is the part that really interests me. When I met and spent time with a psychopath narcissist it was evident to see that this was quite obviously handed down the family line. Now, the big question is this: How did these genetics get there in the first place, and who put them there?

I have a hunch. They are a different strain of human being, one that was created for totally different reasons. These humans are not only missing the empathy code, they're missing an inner moral compass as well. And when it comes to spiritual endeavors, they may have no genuine desire to return to God/Universe/Home, and that is what truly troubles me. It they cannot love, or cannot feel, and recoil from the idea of surrendering to someone or something greater than themselves—how can they have a sincere calling to commune with God and authentically show others the way? As you have probably noticed, it is to the role of "spiritual teacher" that these types tend to be drawn. And of course, they seem quite perfect for the job. My only question is this: What God are they directing people toward?

I have paraphrased the criteria for narcissistic, psychopathic, and sociopathic personality disorders below. Keep in mind that someone can meet many criteria for all of these, as well as other disorders.

NARCISSIST

The narcissist has a principal trait of overvaluing themselves at the expense of devaluing others. They think of themselves as special, privileged, entitled, and void of flaws—in other words, they give themselves plenty of latitude while giving others little to none. In their minds, they are always right, and the rules don't apply to them. They are incapable of admitting mistakes and taking responsibility. If things work, they believe it is thanks to them. If things fail, it's the fault of others.

The following list of narcissistic qualities was adapted from the narcissistic personality disorder criteria in the *Diagnostic and Statistical Manual of Mental Disorders,* fourth edition.* According to the manual, narcissists exhibit a "pervasive pattern of grandiosity . . . need for admiration, and lack of empathy," and these traits are indicated by five or more of the following qualities:

- Has a grandiose sense of self-importance (exaggerates achievements, expects to be recognized as superior without commensurate achievements, etc.)
- Is preoccupied with fantasies of unlimited power, success, brilliance, beauty, or ideal love
- Believes they are "special" and can only be understood by similarly special, high status people
- Requires excessive admiration
- Carries a sense of entitlement
- Is interpersonally exploitative
- Lacks empathy
- Is envious of others or believes others are envious of them
- Shows arrogant, haughty behaviors or attitudes

PSYCHOPATH

The psychopath is callous, cruel, and charming. In fact, you could easily change the name of psychopath to predator and be closer to the truth. They will manipulate others with charisma and intimidation, and can seem to have feelings, but if you look closely—and tune in—these feeling states are not real. It is a pretense, a learned behavior to try to appear normal. The psychopath is calculated and highly organized and can maintain good emotional and physical control in times of stress, threat,

---

*American Psychiatric Society, *Diagnostic and Statistical Manual of Mental Disorders,* 4th ed. with text revision (Washington, DC: American Psychiatric Association Publishing, 2000).

and horror. The psychopath is incredibly aware that what they are doing is wrong and harmful to others, but they do not care. If you imagine a well-dressed, well presented, highly confident person in a position of power surrounded by admiration and fear, that's a psychopath.

Signs of a Psychopath

- Couldn't care less about other people's feelings
- Has no empathy or emotional intelligence
- Puts people's lives in danger and doesn't care
- Does not feel emotions
- Does not accept "no" from anyone, ever
- Is violent and aggressive
- Cannot be stopped from carrying out their agenda
- Believes everyone else is unimportant, stupid, and to be used for their gain
- Would harm their family or anyone who got in the way of their agenda

SOCIOPATH

The sociopath, on the other hand, is less sophisticated than the psychopath. They can appear edgy, nervous, and quick to anger. A sociopath is more likely to spontaneously act out in inappropriate ways. They do not think things through and are often chaotic and recklessly irresponsible. You could say a sociopath is less harmful than the psychopath. If you imagine a hooligan who is in and out of prison regularly and most likely has a drug or alcohol problem—that's a sociopath.

Signs of a Sociopath

- Has superficial charm and reasonable intelligence
- Is prone to delusions and other signs of irrational thinking
- Is prone to nervousness or neurotic behavior
- Is unreliable

- Is dishonest and insincere
- Lacks remorse and shame
- Is inadequately motivated and exhibits antisocial behavior
- Has poor judgment and fails to learn from experience

SPIRITUAL PREDATORS AND PSYCHOPATHS

There are some crystal-clear voices in our community addressing these personality disorders and many other important issues connected with mind-control and hyperdimensional realities. I have asked two exceptional writers/speakers—bodyworker and holistic life-coach Bernhard Guenther and ascension guide, spiritual mentor, and etheric surgeon Lisa Renee—to contribute to this important chapter by adding their flavor to the territory we are crossing with this delicate and explosive subject.

Words from Bernhard Guenther

Bernhard's words are from the post "Spiritual Predators and Pathological Gurus" on his Veil of Reality website.

In light of a recent upsurge in revelations regarding predatory and abusive behavior exhibited by "spiritual" gurus/teachers around the world, I've witnessed two different reactions (generally speaking) to these "unmasking" events. On one hand, many people speak out and help to spread the word about these pathological individuals who have abused their power (usually exhibiting a history of abuse that's been exposed via the many testimonials of brave individuals who chose to come forward). On the other hand, there are people who claim that it is not "spiritual" to "judge" these gurus/teachers, and that the men/women who have accused them are just coming from a place of victim consciousness, projecting their own stuff/wounds/shadow onto the person in question (or they are just engaging in "gossip"), going so far in this approach as to shame/insult the people (victim-blaming) who have stepped forward and shared their stories. Some have even literally stated that they won't read the testimonials/ article in question (motivated reasoning fallacy), and simply defend the guru/teacher in a reflexive manner.

Many of the people who fall into the second category are often-times revealed to be very attached followers of said gurus/teachers (or are part of their "inner circle"). This behavior is a good exam-ple of being caught in group-think and cult-programming mental-ity, which they are obviously not aware of at all. It's the main reason why abuse (sexual, psychological, emotional, physical) in spiritual circles/communities keeps happing [sic] and has been going on for decades—in the case of some "traditions", for centuries. These viola-tions of human sovereignty are usually "swept under the rug" through the abuse (no pun intended) of spiritual "truths" and psychology. It's a form of spiritual bypassing—the worst kind of avoidance—because it not only feeds and fuels more abuse, but justifies it.

In light of this topic and its wider implications, I'd like to address some points about judging, gossip, victim consciousness, shadow pro-jection, making the darkness conscious, pathology, truth and lies, etc.:

Gossip. There is a huge difference between gossip (i.e., "shit talk-ing", malicious rumours, and jealous innuendo), and exposing obvi-ous abuse via the cult behavior/programming of self-proclaimed (pathological) teachers/gurus (based on many testimonials and data spanning over prolonged periods of time).

Gossip is a dualistic virus of petty small-mindedness, founded upon shadow projection to make oneself "feel good" (superior) by talking "bad" about another person based on nothing more than unfounded rumors, assumptions, lies, and accusations. That dis-traction is what "lowers a person's frequency"; and in fact, it is an activity which feeds those occult forces who relish in the narrow-bandwidth frequency of rumour-spreading, and are actively working through those people engaging in it.

Victim/Blame Consciousness. I've written about the trap of victim/blame consciousness before: getting stuck in this very disempowering state can result in severe shadow projection, leading to the hatred of another person (to the point of wanting revenge)—it can lead to distortions/exaggerations, and even the leveling of false accusations. . . .

However, avoiding the trap of victim/blame consciousness does not imply that one should remain silent with regards to suffering abuse at the deeds of a perpetrator/predator. In fact, it is important for the victim to speak out and be heard as part of the healing process, while raising awareness so as to help others. Victim-shaming is a big issue in spiritual circles, most of it based on distorted spiritual truths (which the pathological guru uses, in turn, to "save face" and manipulate his/her followers to defend him/her). This is an ancient game of accountability-avoidance, and relates to the distorted religious program of, *"Whomever is without sin among you, let him be the first to cast stones"*. It's the main reason why pathological "spiritual leaders" have gotten away with abuse—or even justified it amongst their followers—for centuries. It's also one of the reasons why people are afraid to speak out—there are intense emotional programs of guilt/shame attached to such honest courageous openness.

Another way of justifying abuse is the typical, over-simplified misapplication of "It's your Karma" (an inversion of the original Sanskrit meaning, which described the process of sincere self-work, not the subsequent Caste-system-reinforcing fable of reincarnation "consequences"), along with other distorted excuses such as (premature) "Forgiveness", "Law of Attraction", "Unconditional Love", "Truth" and "God's Will". These deflection/"cosmic justification" strawman arguments also usually result in gaslighting the victim.* It also relates

---

*A straw man is a common form of argument and is an informal fallacy based on giving the impression of refuting an opponent's argument, while refuting an argument which was not advanced by that opponent (Source: Wikipedia). Gaslighting is attempting to make someone believe they are going insane. —Ed.

to the watered-down/misinterpreted use of Jungian Psychology, based on the (New Age) fallacy, "when you spot it, you got it", along with, "it's just an expression of all of your wound projections"....

Obviously, none of us are perfect, and we all need to watch out for shadow projections, our tendencies to gossip, or getting caught up in victim/blame mode. But "not being perfect" (i.e. without "sin") does not mean to stay silent/voiceless.

During this Time of Transition any-and-everything is rising from the lurking shadows of our collective unconsciousness. All of it needs to be revealed, examined, healed and transmuted. It's all about making the darkness conscious, and part of this process involves exposing lies, corruption and pathology. This is NOT about being "negative", nor does it "lower" one's frequency. It's about accountability, integrity, and responsibility and giving the lie what it deserves: the truth.

Keep in mind that ALL there is out here (from a soul evolutionary perspective) in the realm of material existence are lessons, and even the pathological guru/teacher predator serves a "teaching function": it asks a person to reclaim their own power and sovereignty, without giving it away to anyone or any group, and to avoid putting anyone on a pedestal....

Psycho-Pathology. It's very important to understand that "we" are not all the same. There are pathological individuals (Narcissists, Sociopaths, Psychopaths) who operate very differently than most "normal" human beings, but perform behind a well-crafted "mask of sanity." They can have very high IQs, exude self-confidence, express themselves eloquently, and can even possess certain "powers" to heal AND manipulate others, while emulating and mimicking "spiritual wisdom," "empathy" and "love" quite well, without truly meaning, embodying, or feeling any of it. In fact, it is very hard to spot high-functioning psychopaths right away, due to their experience with self-camouflage.

That's why a basic understanding of Psychopathology is a key resource to possess in this day and age, especially within spiritual circles/communities. One must understand how the wolf in sheep's clothing operates—to be able to see through their "mask of sanity". . . .

The lack of understanding surrounding basic psycho-pathology—or even basic psychology and cult-psychology—is a primary reason why so many well-meaning (wounded) people get so easily trapped/abused in cult-like group dynamics, and it's also why dedicated followers of such predators keep defending him/her, because they are still under his/her "spell", mimicking/repeating the same distorted "spiritual truths". . . .

Also keep in mind that a full-blown Narcissist/Sociopath/Psychopath will never be able to truly own his/her stuff, nor feel any remorse for their abuses, nor take true responsibility for his/her actions. He/she may engage in superficial apologetic behaviors that are not sincere; given that these types are pathological liars and master manipulators, you cannot expect to reason with them nor make them "see" the truth. It's not that they don't want to do so—they simply can't actualize such a process. The only way out, so to speak, is to establish CLEAR boundaries, and disengage from the previous relational situation. . . .

Truth Is Mixed with Lies. Another big issue I've observed is that followers of pathological gurus/teachers who come out to his/her defense oftentimes claim that his/her work/teachings has helped them tremendously in their process and healing journey, and hence, there can't be anything wrong with them as individuals/mentors. First of all, this is actually a very selfish/narcissistic tactic on the part of the follower, because it's re-framing the conversation around "their process" and eliminating the voice of the brave individuals who have come forward with their testimonials of abuse. Secondly, it may well be the truth that some aspects of the guru/teacher's work/teachings have helped them, but this does not automatically imply that all is fine and good with regard to the personal actions of the healer/teacher, and no abuse has happened with other clients/

students (it's actually a "red herring" . . . logical fallacy, which goes back to the last point about critical thinking).

In Psychological Manipulation programs, truth is often mixed with lies, and powerful/pathological gurus/teachers who claim to have "special knowledge" and "powers" will deploy "truths" in order to lure the seeker into their grip, and then distort said truth enough to keep them entrapped in their game, especially when there's an established hierarchy (and inside competition between followers who want to get closer to the guru/teacher). It's also an ancient game which relates to the esoteric saying, *"Satan most often appears as an angel of light."*

Good (as in "effective") disinformation is a potent combination of empowerment and deception, most often packaged as a high percentage of truth (or imitation of truth) to lure the seeker in, only for them to be "undone" by the underlying foundation of lies. The falsehoods are usually designed so as to undermine the "window dressing" truth, vector the undiscerning seeker away from uncovering more truth for themselves, and to make him/her take a detour off their own path as they get lost in the cult-ish labyrinth (while believing themselves to be on the right track).

Not Talking Negatively about Others. This relates to the first point, above, with regards to mistakenly conflating the exposure of pathological behavior/abuse with gossiping or "judgmental" negativity. It is directly tied into the typical New Age fallacy which preaches that we should all "just focus on the positive and ignore the negative". . . .

There is this contrived "niceness" in today's "conscious movements", where people don't want to say anything "negative" (in their subjective understanding of it, of course). In general, some folks hide behind a "social etiquette" mask, without wanting to say anything "bad" or touching on any "taboo subjects". They speak around issues in order to be spiritually or politically "correct" so as to "not step on anyone's toes". . . .

This attitude of contrived "niceness" essentially creates the conditions for conformity, complacency, ignorance and the atrophy of critical thinking. . . .

Personal Sovereignty. We need be become our own personal leaders and internal authorities, learning to trust ourselves and our own power in the process instead of giving it away to anyone else; therein lies the development of true spiritual sovereignty. Many people have the need to follow some "figurehead", be it a government "personality", medical professional or spiritual guru. Individuals oftentimes get sucked into the "celebrity matrix" and latch onto authors and researchers they admire as well, blindly following what they say without doing their own fact-checking or listening to their bodily intuition. There is a big difference between getting inspired by people who put out work that resonates with us (and from whom we can learn new points of view) and putting those same folks on a pedestal, living only by the content of what they publish without questioning it at all, and projecting absolute authority onto them, whether it's done consciously or not.

The latter situation is how we wind up getting cut off from our own inner knowing intuition guidance system—the "network" which holds our personal truth that is unique to us, and which lights up our individual path and illuminates our life lessons. When we abdicate personal accountability to sovereign thought and deed, it puts us into a tunnel vision situation which actually disconnects us from our divine nature and innate wisdom. It is about simultaneously recognizing and honoring both our individuality and our inter-connectedness, relating with others and striving for community but not getting lost in self-limiting group/hive mind thinking.

Always think for yourself, never follow anyone blindly, and never fall into an unquestioning mindset, no matter how charismatic or "wise" your heroes may appear to be. Never give in to group and peer pressure if it contradicts your own experience, intuition, and research.*

Words from Lisa Renee

Lisa's words come from the post "Lying Techniques" on her Energetic Synthesis website.

It is important to be able to identify abusers, liars, predators and psychopaths as people traumatized by terrible pain, soul fragmentation and spiritual disconnection. When people are utterly controlled by negative ego dysfunction and have no impulse control and they live in self-deception. A person who is deceiving themselves has no other alternative but to deceive others because they have little to no clarity.

As we build better and practical ways of discerning trustworthiness and competency, we also gain confidence to build stronger intuition in such matters, where the checklist is not required. As is made clear here in these checklists, the more severe the Negative Ego dysfunction the more potentially disconnected the person is from their heart, intuition, self-awareness and spiritual source. This immediately gives one a gauge to measure what level a person can be trusted, no matter what words they may be speaking.

In the severe stages of Narcissism and Psychopathy, the veneer of seduction, charisma and "mimicry" of empathic reactions that are geared for manipulation to serve one's egocentric needs, and can be seen much more clearly over time. It is very common for people that base their leadership or authority on controlling behaviors and tyrannical principles, to aggressively manipulate others by creating a façade of charisma by mimicking what they have found people want to hear from their wounded ego parts.

---

*Bernhard Guenther, "Spiritual Predators and Pathological Gurus," Veil of Reality (website), December 27, 2018.

Many people do not want to hear or know the truth; they want to be lulled to sleep by fantasy delusions. Megalomaniacs that thrive on taking power and having control over others, are master manipulators of telling people lies based on what they want to hear or believe.

This is the tough part. We have to ask if we are able to seek the honest factual truth of behavioral interactions or have people feed us lies that are flattering or comfortable for our wounded ego parts.

Otherwise, we reinforce the delusion in the person/circumstance and we become enablers, allowing them to continue to perpetrate deceptions in the group through their own self-deception. Promoting and enabling delusions leads to pathological thinking and spreads a fabricated reality through "false impressions". This false impression is the spin on perceptions that are designed to serve the agenda of the ego, narcissistic or psychopath.*

Time and consistency will always reveal to you the truth in the matter, if you are willing to patiently seek the truth rather than remaining in denial because it feels more comfortable. As we improve our skills for identifying these harmful behaviors and stop feeding them, we can also connect the dots to see the direct relationship these behaviors have to the Archonic Deception strategies used to weaken and control human beings.

So, after reading Bernard and Lisa's wisdom, you're probably wondering how to cut loose from these kinds of people and circumstances? The problem is, this energy is not only on the outside; it's on the inside too. We are the piggy in the middle, or the bridge to the most high. But first, one step at a time:

> Step 1: Be aware.
> Step 2: Get out.
> Step 3: Inform others.

---

*Lisa Renee, "Lying Techniques," Energetic Synthesis (website).

EIGHT WAYS TO PULL THE PLUG
ON THE PREDATOR

Like it or not, the era of transparency is coming! All that was hidden is now being seen, as the vows of silence get broken and the lid gets lifted from Pandora's box. For so long people—women mostly—have kept silent about their intuitive hunches in their workplace, families, and communities. But this is changing. Like a series of dominoes, as one woman speaks, she gives permission to her sister to do the same.

In 2017, we saw the sex scandal of Harvey Weinstein come to light. A famous Hollywood film director was exposed by a large number of women coming forward to say they were sexually harassed or assaulted by Weinstein—allegations he denied.

A year later, spirituality followed the same rigorous exposé. And it was about time. What we need to highlight is how the spiritual community hides its many skeletons—not only the mess caused by teachers sleeping with their students, but the threats and isolation that occurs should anyone tell the truth. Woven within these covert communities is the pressure to hand over money, sell property, keep vows of silence, and agree not to learn from any other source, and often followers are brainwashed into believing families, friends, and even other students are under the influence of negative forces. Slowly, slowly we are broken down as we enter the spell and freely offer up our own sovereign, free-thinking, intuitive self.

Everyone else outside of the community can clearly see and feel what is going on. That is why we are strongly urged to separate from these people. This could easily include our own children, spouse, previous teachers, best friends, and even animal companions!

Perhaps you've already broken away and are wondering why your whole life is upside down, and you're finding it extremely difficult to trust anything again. Be patient. I have been there. We do heal; it simply takes time.

Or if you're not quite there yet but have been lucky enough to pay attention to your hunches and correctly question the validity of what you are getting involved in, below is an eight-step process for executing a plan to leave these influences behind.

As you take these steps, remember that you may be in a broken and fragile state, you may have been compromised. Your trust may have been torn to pieces, and your mind filled with illusions. Gently, gently, gently you can find your true heart and natural ways to heal. Seek out goodness, welcome laughter, keep it simple, and you shall be reborn.

1. Decide to Leave and *Get Out.* Just leave. Now. Pack what you can and walk out the door. Just go. I left with only the clothes on my back and the equivalent of $9 in my pocket. Once you leave, everything begins to change. This is what breaks the spell.

2. Close Every Form of Communication. Block the predator on Facebook, email, telephone, Google—everything. Don't forget the inner circle, the people who cocoon the predator and administer his/her lies and veils. *Never* trust the inner circle. Usually these people are women and are not to be believed. Block them also.

3. Reconnect with Trusted Friends and Family. You will need good old-fashioned friends who know and love you dearly to be around as you slowly start the process of finding your true Self again. These people must not judge or question you—yet. You need only to be held and to feel safe.

4. Begin Your Healing Process Naturally. Do *not* take on another teacher. Avoid energy work too soon. Do *not* start looking for answers. First, rest. Unwind. Sleep. You must find your Self on the inside and gently ease yourself back into the body.

5. Learn to Trust Again. Who and what can you trust after an experience like this? It's not easy, but it must be done if you wish to experience a good and wholesome life. I started with animals. Then it was yoga. I trusted my body and my breath. When I finally got the courage to go outside, I trusted nature.

6. Restore Your Intuition. Now would be the time to begin some energy work once you have elements of your Self and trust back. Begin practices and processes that awaken and strengthen your intuition. Strike up a dialogue. Record your findings. With reverence, approach your inner Self and gently ask, "What was the purpose of meeting this person? And why did I attract this experience? What more can I heal?"

7. Source from Truth/Love/Joy. And now for the difficult part— finding God/faith again. This was incredibly difficult for me as my inner world felt violated, polluted, and broken. But there must be a time when you venture back into the Self and begin to pray. Slowly, humbly, and with great care for your bruised and battered self, feel into the source of your being. Find your sacred origins and rest there. No need for any big conversations. Simply rest in union with your quiet and eternal Self.

And then comes the crown of the experience:

8. Claim the Antidote—the Awareness and Ability to Inform Others. Name it, sister/brother! Spill the beans. Break the vow of silence. Grant yourself the permission and power to speak up about your experiences and inform others. This kind of corruption thrives on silence and fear by disempowering others. Break the spell. Speak out.

HOW THE INNER PREDATOR GETS FORMED

Here is where we must look inside and ask ourselves some uncomfortable but essential questions. If we have attracted a predator into our lives, is there something within that wanted or rather needed to experience that encounter? Those of us who have an inner predator would have had some severe trauma in our childhood that set us up for repeating the trauma in a similar form. Mysteriously, the psyche does this to protect itself from further harm while inflicting it again and again. It is probable that our false guru/husband/sister etc. (whomever was/is the outer predator) was also traumatized as a child by some predator-like experience with a relative or someone they trusted. Those who are wounded in this way are usually attracted to each other.

The great work here for us is to transform our *inner* predator into a helper, an ally. Usually, for a woman, the predator is male and is what Carl Jung called her "animus," or her unconscious masculine side. A negative animus can destroy a woman, but he can be transformed into a positive, helpful animus by making his voice conscious. What he is asking for is a relationship with the woman. He is part of her wholeness and can help her manifest her feeling values in the world. He originates in a childhood wound that is asking for healing. He really represents the wounded aspect of her Soul. The gift is healing.

The heart is like an umbilical cord that unites our inner and outer worlds. It extends itself out into the exterior world innocently connecting with others, places, and spaces like a wondrous child excited to play. It also reaches deep within to keep safe our innermost sanctum and the grace we have been given to live. What we must realize is how sensitive the heart is, especially in our young and formative years. Anything that happens "out there" is also deeply felt "in here." There is no barrier when we are a child, no constructed armor or defense. So the older we get the more wounds our heart carries, and this eventually, over time, impairs our physical and psychic wellness.

It's during these delicate and tender years that the inner predator gets formed. A trauma so powerful in feeling shocks the heart out of kilter and in that schism, the predator is born. The abrasive heartache of endless hot tears, rocking back and forth in search of comfort and huddling yourself together to soothe your terror is the birthing bed of the most frightening force you will ever, ever encounter.

What we must realize is that this was born within us, to protect us. If only at that moment we knew this and welcomed it in. Usually, we sense its ferocious nature and cut ourselves away, pushing it further into the subconscious where it grows and develops into an anti-love force capable of anything. Conceived out of our screams, it is insistent on hunting us down. It carries the fragments of our Soul, splintered by terror. The more it chases us, the more we run; the more we run, the more frustrated it becomes. All it wants to do is bring us back into wholeness. The frustration turns in on itself and twists into a white rage, mad with hysteria and chaos. Now we have a real nemesis inside of us. All we can do is condone it as evil and plan our many ways to get rid of it. Now, who is the real predator?

I have an inner predator. I came into contact with this when I was a child. I have also met the inner predator in the external world. Now, after all these years have passed, my inner predator has become my ally. That doesn't mean everything is happy-go-lucky. It means I must stay vigilant, sovereign, and genuinely connected to my origins, at all times, leaving no crack for any kind of influence to come in and take over.

I hope this information has illuminated and confirmed what you have quietly known all this time, and despite its message, has liberated you in a true and lasting way.

Overpopulation

There's an incredibly obvious problem going on in our world that I don't see or hear many people talking about: overpopulation. This may be one of the main reasons, if not *the* main reason, for all of the other Sorrows of the World.

There are too many of us on this planet. And we need feeding. And we need land to grow our food and store our animal products. And we need water for ourselves, our crops, and our animal products. And we need shelter, and we need power, and we need transportation, and we need, and we need, and we need . . .

And still, we keep on multiplying. We are classified as mammals, yet all other mammals instinctively develop a natural equilibrium with their surrounding environment. But we do not. We move to an area and multiply and multiply until every natural resource is consumed and the only way we can survive is to spread to another area. There is another organism on this planet that follows the same pattern, and that's a virus. And to think that we call ourselves advanced!

Take a look around. Is this true?

Overpopulation is an undesirable condition where the number of existing humans exceeds the carrying capacity of Earth. Overpopulation is caused by a number of factors such as reduced mortality rate, better medical facilities, and technological advancement in fertility treatments.

I know it's not a popular subject—but is anyone else addressing this?

I'm going to take a chance right now and suggest a conscious solution. Already I can hear the many voices of opposition. But it's nowhere near as loud as the voice that says to me, *you must write this.*

I would propose an immediate one-child maximum legislation. After that, there's a conscious and responsible approach to lovemaking, and no additional children are conceived. The desire to have "just one more child" is offered up to the greater cause of working together to bring this glorious planet back into equilibrium and harmony.

Should there be another pregnancy, a responsible natural solution is taken to ensure the release of the potential of that child as a ritual to offer further sustenance to the earth. I believe it has to be seen and approached in this conscious, loving, and responsible way.

A second step would be to empower and educate women (and men) across the globe of the problems we face and the heartfelt reasons why contraception and family planning are essential. We must create a worldwide community of women working together and supporting one another to ensure the availability of empowerment, education, contraception, doulas, and womb wives (women who perform womb rites and rituals).

A third step would be a government incentive to strengthen responsible parenthood by financially supporting and investing in both adult and child education. This could be done by integrating lessons on population, environment, and development into the school curriculum at multiple levels. The main purpose of this is to reunite us with the natural world and to establish the desire to create careers and jobs in the environmental industry.

Finally, the last step would be an immediate worldwide conscription, a compulsory enlistment of people in a national service to assist with the cleanup of the planet. This program would be seen and felt as a joyful, purposeful contribution to the community, rather than a heavy burden.

Someone's got to say it . . .

Pause here for reflection. Take the time that is needed to truly be with these insights and understandings. Just breathe and be with them. Let's bear witness to the sobriety of the situation and feel one another as we rise together to receive more of Her transmission.

Let's move on without answers.

We must learn to trust the process, remembering that *this is an initiation.*

ELEVEN
Breaking Our Silence

THE FEMININE HAS BEEN SO DISEMPOWERED, separated from her true and protective voice. Her voice is the custodian of the natural world, and for so long, we have been sitting back, silently agonizing over the genocide all around us, grasping at our throats and silently screaming like banshees. Our volume has been turned down by the Dark Agenda via a lethal cocktail of vanity and greed. We have been encouraged to be perfect, pleasing, pretty, and passive. Our men have gone along with the program, believing that women equal sex and sex equals power.

All the while, we've been acting out our own Roman orgy; the human population has exploded to levels that simply cannot be sustained. We have multiplied and multiplied and multiplied again, and now there are 7.6 billion of us on the planet, breathing, eating, consuming, defecating, discarding, and dying. While all this mindless fuckery carries on, the Earth heats up, the jungles are torn down, the oceans become devoid of fish, animals are slaughtered for consumption or become extinct because of game sports, and that 7.6 billion figure suddenly becomes 10 billion. With 10 billion people on the planet, we would be at the uppermost population limit as far as food is concerned, and 70 percent of the Earth would have to be used to produce food.

Our planet will become a farm. A place to grow food—exclusively.

The bitter pill we may all have to swallow is that this global problem cannot be solved. Even though the solutions have been readily available, the conditions to implement them have not. By 2020 population growth could cause two-thirds of all wildlife to disappear.* And I've already noted the possibility of no fish left in the sea by 2048. Beloved friends, the collapse of the natural world is coming much faster than even the doomsayers are predicting. These are not only the failings of our specific time in history, they are the hallmarks of a civilization at the end of its cycle.

All that is left is to ensure as much as possible that we leave the planet in a position where it is still able to sustain itself and evolve new life. What matters most for us now is not the outcome of our efforts but rather our innermost intentions. We may be powerless to reverse the situation, but we are not powerless to create sanctuaries of peace, we are not powerless to speak truth to people, and we are not powerless to prepare ourselves and heal ourselves with the diligence that will be needed amid a sea of change.

We must break our silence. We must say what the people most need to hear. No more secrets. No more silence. No more fear.

Here we are yet again at a familiar and uncomfortable threshold: finding the ability to speak truth to power. I suspect it has been a long time—if ever—since we, the feminine, were able to speak fearlessly, clearly, and directly to whomever and whatever. Now that we teeter on the unknown edge of retrieving our voices, we can often feel a sense of dread of and heated resistance to speaking the truth to just about anyone.

If you don't yet believe me, let's agree to tell the truth for the next three days to absolutely everyone that we come into contact with, online and in real life. This includes the truth of our thoughts, feelings, and actions. Maybe within these three days, there will be an opportunity to speak to a situation that you have observed that simply isn't right to ignore or brush aside. This is where I personally feel my conditioning the most, being brave enough to speak up in public when it apparently isn't my business. For example, this might be when I observe a person hitting or treating their dog or horse harshly. The same with a child,

---

*Brian Clark Howard, "World to Lose Two-Thirds of Wild Animals by 2020?" National Geographic (website), October 27, 2016.

or a woman. It's that moment, when we allow that rising heat of Kali to make it all the way to our heart and voice so She can intervene and bring justice to a cruel and bullying situation.

As I wrote this chapter I was steered in the direction of the many, many atrocities that still to this day are happening against women. I read their stories and bore witness to their videos. I want to share with you the horrors that are still taking place in the world where men rule, and anything—anything—can be done to a woman. Because within us, beloved women, we know, we feel, we sense, and we hear the voices of all women, and it's terrifying that we live in a place where these things can happen, where these things *are* happening. Womankind and the feminine essence has a predator and it lives on the inside and the outside. It threatens to hunt her should she become free; it threatens to torture her should she grow strong; and it threatens to silence her should she speak up. This age-long fear that can silence us for centuries, and most certainly has, must cease to be. The predator on the inside has been formed by the predator on the outside. As we found out in the Bluebeard story, the pent-up anguish along with living in fear of repetitive violence, aggression, and/or rape all pool together to birth an entity made up of the silent screams, rage, and grief at our ordeal. Therefore, I am including a real-life story of Soraya M., not only because I want to make sure this woman and the many, many others do not die or endure this level of insane horror in vain but also for us all to meet the living predator within patriarchy and understand why we must now break our silence.

THE STONING OF SORAYA M

It is always moving when women are the subjects of their own stories. Sometimes its uplifting, other times its thought-provoking. I have not chosen this story to shock but rather to bear witness to the horrors sometimes inflicted upon women, so that we might vicariously feel an infinitesimal fraction of their suffering. If we feel this, perhaps it will motivate us to ensure that their voices are heard.

Soraya M as portrayed in the film *The Stoning of Soraya M*

The Stoning of Soraya M, a film based on the book *La Femme Lapidée,* is based on the true story of a woman framed for adultery by her husband and her subsequent inhumane execution at the hands of her entire village. It puts a name and a story to what would otherwise purely be a statistic. The film has since been banned in Iran, the country this true story came from. What message do governments send to their people and to the world about their approach to human rights when they shut out women's stories in this manner? What message do they send to other women in society and, most crucially of all, to other potential perpetrators of these abuses?

In this story, one woman is convicted by a group of men for a fabricated crime. Then as punishment for that crime, she is tied up and buried up to her waist, defenseless, while another group, consisting largely of men, throw stones at her from a distance. Imagine now that our own community has a gathering at the local park this weekend. All of our friends and neighbors have been invited to the big event. The woman down the street has been accused of adultery by her husband and three of his friends, so she has been sentenced to death by stoning.

In the middle of the field, a woman we know is buried in the ground up to her chest and everyone is circled around her. There are piles of stones ready to be thrown. These stones are large enough that they will cause life-ending damage, but not too big to kill her on impact. The stoning is meant to be a slow, painful, and deliberate death.

Her husband has the "honor" of throwing the first stone. Then her sons are coaxed into taking part. They are told to do it for God. The woman is allowed to try and escape, but she is buried too deeply. For the next ten to twenty minutes the rest of our community joins in until there is nothing left but a bloody stump.

If there is any act more cowardly and inhumane than this, it's hard to imagine, though the following does come close. Another group, consisting largely of men with the power to make the changes this time, decided that the story shouldn't be heard and that the film should be banned.

It's one thing for a rogue group of individuals to commit a heinous human rights crime. It's quite another to see this level of spinelessness multiplied on an institutional level. We can't fight human rights abuses if those with authority don't do all they can to stand as visibly as possible in solidarity with the victims.

We must remember that these human rights abuses are worldwide, and we need to amplify the voices of the silenced people and listen to their stories as carefully as we can. Should you read the book or watch the movie, please don't turn away. It's people turning away and refusing to understand what a stoning truly means, what it truly does to a human body—a human being—that these hideous events are permitted to continue.

The stoning does not stop because the person is dead. It continues until there is nothing left except something completely unrecognizable.

These stories and the many like them have contributed to the psychic gag around our mouths. Deep inside we know these things are taking place, even now; in this moment women are being captured, tortured, starved, beaten, mutilated, and fed their own child as a demented form of hellish punishment. These real-life stories and the sickening dread of knowing them create the 101 reasons to remain silent, submissive, and dress up as a patriarchy plaything. In one half of the world, women are brainwashed into being all tits and ass, whereas on the other side of the planet females are tortured, maimed, and killed for fear of the same behavior. This is what distracts us. This game created and kept going by patriarchy's major hang-ups around the feminine.

Are we, women, going to continue being rag dolls that are pushed and pulled in every direction, rather than the most important one? Can't we see that we have been hoodwinked into submission, distracted from our role of caretaker of the patch of land known as our garden, our neighborhood, our village, and our city? We have become preoccupied with pleasing our fathers, dressing for our husbands, mollycoddling our sons, learning to fit in or trying everything to stand out. Fuck that. Somewhere in the middle is Truth. Somewhere way beyond patriarchy's mind warp of twisted sickness is the elegance, dignity, and beauty of a free woman.

What is it that creates her beauty? Freedom from the game. She dresses for no one but herself. Her false seductions and charms are thrown to the floor, seen for what they truly are—pocket money to feed the death wish of the Dark Agenda. Suddenly she can see the falsity she has lived under, how she has danced for the warmongering scoundrels, getting down on her knees for a few pieces of loose change flung at her for her efforts. Hanging around for a few compliments and hopefully a leg up on the career ladder or a fancy home she can be proud of, while the ocean is emptied of fish and a nuclear bomb is dangerously close to being launched.

These superficial trivialities are not important. Not now. Not that they ever were. But what is important is who we are going to become in this devastating time. And what can we do/be together to ensure a life-giving planet long after we have gone?

BREAKING MY SILENCE

During the writing of *Fierce Feminine Rising,* I noticed this constant feeling of growing unrest. I thought, at first, it was the material that was being covered in this book. That would make sense considering all the highly controversial veils that were being lifted. But that was not it.

As I accessed more and more stories and studies of what was happening on our planet and inside our own heads, little did I know that I too was being prepped and readied for the genuine embodiment of this Divine and holy force.

I was only three months into writing the book when my personal opportunity to stand as the Fierce Feminine appeared before me. It was in that moment that I realized that in my writing and your reading of this book, we will each be given an initiatory experience that unites us with the countless others that are embodying the resilience of the Dark Mother in this time. And so I took this opportunity with both hands to break my silence about the things that happened to me in my past, because those same things were clearly still happening to others in the present.

It all happened so fast as if Divinely orchestrated, which it was. Before I knew it, I was part of a growing group of others that were coming out and notifying our community of a dangerous predatory spiritual teacher that was resistant to change. One of the strongest components to this speaking up activity was that we were a group. It must be even harder, if not impossible, to be the only one to speak the truth. I believe our strength this time was in our numbers and the commitment to not bail out but to see it through to the very end. It was this level of integrity and accountability that gave us the confidence to stand strong and resist the backlash that would inevitably come our way.

In our circle, we gave one another the permission and power to speak up and out about issues that no doubt would have haunted our ancestors with a silence that was deathly and enforced. But we didn't do that. Together, we broke the mold and patiently held sacred space around each person as they prepared the testimony of their ordeal with the same spiritual teacher. With wise eyes and compassionate hearts, we read one another's words, making sure each person was standing in their power and was not coming from a place of victimhood or vengeance. Together we cleaned, polished, and presented our truth, seeing and owning all the components that made up our shared experience. We encouraged one another to get crystal clear and precise with our Soul's wisdom, to unite with truth before speaking it out. It was only from that united place that we presented our testimonials, at a moment that was so healing, and clearly strewn with grace and Divine timing.

There were many times when I could have easily backed down and walked away. I could have convinced myself to pass the buck onto some other person—someone younger, gutsier, or whoever else I could use to fit the excuse I was making. I could have simply hoped they would have the bravery to do what I couldn't, but I didn't. And I thank God every day that I persevered.

Speaking truth out into the world is not easy, as it often gets met with resistance, judgment, and hostility. When we speak up and out for the first time we are usually filled with the hope that our words could fall on receptive ears and that perhaps some radical shift will get made. What is more likely to happen at first, until truth is not feared anymore, is that it will get met with an energy that is incapable of hearing it, incapable of holding it, and more importantly, incapable of responding to it. But we cannot let that put us off because we never know where and how our truth will be received. We never know who will read it, who will hear it, and what may become of it as we let go. We have agreed to be the forerunners, we have remembered our yes, our willingness to be awake and to throw caution to the wind, allowing our acorns of truth to drop wherever they will. At first, this might seem hard, we may feel disappointed, disillusioned, and deflated, as nothing much appears to be happening. But don't let that discourage you, this is how it is for pioneering spirits. At first, a species must experience an impulse to change, then after a long period of carrying that impulse, there is a transformation.

Let us not be concerned about how our truth is received; what matters is that we speak it. Our duty is only to speak the truth and let the people decide what they want to do with it. It has been my experience that when we do come out and reveal the truth, there is often a strong sense of judgment in response, as there are always some who simply do not want to hear what we're saying. They may be angry at us for raising the subject, feeling threatened by our words and the new position we hold. There will, of course, be others who are grateful that we have finally found the courage to speak out because it's what they suspected all along.

My other piece of advice is to not take any of the backlash personally. This is not about you; it's about how they feel in response to the truth, which they most likely already know in their heart of hearts. Should you be in a position where you need to break your silence on an important and far-reaching situation, make sure you get totally clear. Take your time and feel into your heart and Soul before you do or say anything. Once you have reached that inner sanctuary, then from that place speak up and out.

Should you experience a backlash of judgment or accusation, return to any of the transmissions included in this book, especially when you are feeling hounded, falsely accused, and isolated. The transmissions carry a frequency that can compassionately meet this place inside of you and transmute all of your fears and doubt into even more clarity and bravery for what you're being asked to stand for.

When I broke my silence, I used the online world as my platform. I intuitively knew to deliver the message and get it out. I did not spend any of my time looking at the comments, let alone reading them. I knew that these messages whether they be positive or negative would be an enticement to once again enter the drama. By this time, I had enough years under my belt to know exactly where that drama begins and ends, and it is of no interest to me anymore. I believe it is important for our day-to-day life to be rooted in the physical, the family, the relational, and the regular tasks of everyday living. The online world is a breeding ground for all kinds of frequencies and intentions. It is the perfect platform for things to get amplified, coerced, misunderstood, manipulated, and downright made up.

We must be clear, my friends, so crystal clear on every single level. We must be clear with our parents, clear with our children, clear with our partners, and clear with our work. We also have to be clear with the things we're saying yes to and the things we're saying no to. There can be no outstanding debt of any kind. I don't mean only a financial debt, but every type of contract, agreement, interaction, etc. Every exchange must be cleanly administered and ended when complete. It is when we begin to accrue energetic debt that energy starts to gather and create deadly and dangerous offspring. It is when things are messy, dishonorable, neglectful, and ignored that the forces of the Dark Agenda can begin to creep in. Using the cracks in our integrity, the shadows form, creating a smorgasbord of intensely felt emotions and reactions, when it could have been a simple and honest human matter.

We must be able to discern quite clearly where our energy is being placed and whether we are in full agreement to it. This is one way we can avoid these toxic entanglements and the kind of territories they lead us into. We must take our time to feel into all the invitations that come our way and not be hassled and hustled by life, so we can cleanly and full-heartedly say yes or no.

Once you make your decision and decide to step over that threshold inside of yourself that says you can't possibly say this or bring this up, and when you make a clean and centered decision to do exactly that, I promise that you will be met with an embrace that is safe and supportive. This embrace is from another part of you that has been patiently waiting for you to do this all along. It's as if you have stepped into the man or woman you were always meant to become. You may fear that it could be a step off into the abyss and into aloneness, but it isn't. It's a good first step out of the controlled and frightened you, into an awake and fearlessly free part of yourself. This part of you, that you sort of recognize, produces all kinds of synchronistic events and circumstances that support and develop what it is you are standing for. Suddenly you become thrust into another world that kind of looks the same but is shining gloriously with good energy and intent.

You have said no to being silent.

You are Divine, and now more than ever you truly need to reach for this and live it. Stay awake. Use your voice wisely. No one has the power to silence you; not now, not ever.

Transmission
Free Our Voice*

We are not obliged to live under the law of man, only the law of nature. When we truly feel that, when we truly know that natural law is our only governing force, we can inwardly remove any symbolic obstacle that has silenced us. This may be a gag, a noose, a shadow at our back, or the removal of our tongue. Remember, it's an energetic symbol. Who knows what or who placed it there. With great reverence and heart-centered authority, we can remove it and discard it outside of our auric field, making sure we transmute it into something beautiful and natural before it leaves us. In that way, we are energetically cleaning our debris, and not expecting the imaginative realm of the fifth dimension to take care of things.

Come into a comfortable seated position with your eyes closed. Take this moment to center yourself deep in your body. Come to the midline, the balance point of out there and in here. Rest here awhile in connection with who you are in the world, and what you are in the inner realms. Collect and gather yourself together, using the breath to collate and establish harmony. When you feel ready, solemnly agree to stop being a plaything for the patriarchy. Placing your hand on your heart, align with sovereignty. Whatever the external world of events and circumstances bring, remain true and free to speak that truth.

---

*An audio track of this meditative exercise can be downloaded at audio.innertraditions .com/fiferi.

Touch your throat and grant yourself the permission to speak truth and the choices needed to maintain that truth. Witness your transformation as you notice the subtle tingling animations within the vocal cords and mouth. It is in doing this that you connect your voice to the seat of your intuition, and the fire within your heart.

When you feel ready, turn in your ancestral line to face your mother. See her own symbolic silence and wait until you feel compassion for her arise in your heart. Then remove her silence in the same way, transmuting it into a harmonic tonic for the natural world. Continue to witness how your mother turns to her mother, your grandmother, and performs the same gesture of liberating her voice. On and on, back through the records of time, the girls and women in our ancestral line turn to face their mothers as they remove the ancient blood-soaked rags from their lips. Witness and enshrine this reality into your heart as you establish this new truth into your DNA.

Overproduction

It is with such a heavy heart that I sit down and speak on this Sorrow of the World that is yet another example of greed and the distortion that exists in our world.

Farmers are overproducing both crops and animal products. Fishermen are overfishing and sending the dead fish back into the sea. Car manufacturers produce cars that no one buys. Clothes are being made that no one needs, food gets bought and made that doesn't get eaten, and TV shows get recorded that never get watched.

There is nothing more wasteful than producing something no one wants. And yet there are people on this planet who are hungry, surviving on less than a dollar a day, and living in shelters that we wouldn't expect our animals to sleep in.

I am shaking my head in total despair.

Apparently, there's a natural drive in humanity to overproduce.

Darwin was reported to have said that "overproduction happens when species reproduce many more offspring than can possibly survive." The problem is, *we are* surviving, along with all of the stuff that we make that no one else wants or needs.

I am certain that this natural drive to overproduce is coming from our loss of connection to our Souls. If we were a species that was inherently at peace with the world, we would never overproduce, and we would not allow others to do so either, as there's no purpose in it.

But there is no point in my or anyone else's ranting now. Let's instead look to a solution.

First, we must realize that this problem is twofold: With overproduction comes an escalating rise in waste. If we produce too much, we then have to get rid of it. And because we have most likely made it out of nonrecyclable materials, it is toxic and never actually goes away, which causes huge, negative environmental impact and serious problems.

This is a monster of a problem, but we can figure it out if we do it together. It's easy to despair at the scale of the task, but it isn't beyond humanity to solve it. Manufacturers got us into this mess, and our governments should take responsibility for allowing it. However, we cannot undo what has already been created. So, first and foremost, overproduction and excessive buying must stop—now! We must increase our accountability and responsibility for what we are buying and continuing to be part of. If we go shopping, let's not bring home a problem.

We must also transform our attitudes of entitlement and privilege to necessity and modesty, from carelessly throwing away to reducing, reusing, and recycling. Much like with overpopulation, I believe the government needs to impose an immediate worldwide conscription, a compulsory enlistment of people in a national service to assist with the cleanup of the planet. A friend of mine shared with me a great idea that is growing in and around London. Apparently, individuals are starting to remove all of the packaging at the checkout counter and leaving it there. It is a nonharmful protest and it's getting the point across quite sharply. This way, the supermarkets will have to take notice.

We all have to, and soon.

Pause here for reflection. Take the time that is needed to truly be with these insights and understandings. Just breathe and be with them. Let's bear witness to the sobriety of the situation and feel one another as we rise together to receive more of Her transmission.

Let's move on without answers.

We must learn to trust the process, remembering that *this is an initiation.*

TWELVE
She Who Knows

A FEW MONTHS AGO, I watched a TalkWorks interview with Anne Baring, a Jungian analyst and author from the United Kingdom, discussing the splitting of the atom and the loss of the deep feminine. This subject matter greatly inspired me, and I found myself contemplating its deeper meaning in the days and weeks that followed.

Anne made it clear that the splitting of the atom caused a simultaneous split within our own psyche. That at its root, this desire to split matter was coming from a fundamental schism caused by religion, which implied that matter was contaminated (since the fall of our world) and that we humans could treat matter, and therefore nature, any way we wanted since it was seen as an inferior substance. The moment we split the atom was the exact moment we plunged into an even deeper sense of irreparable and nonnegotiable separation.

> *Although contemporary man believes that he can change himself without limit, the astounding or rather terrifying fact remains that despite civilization and the influence of religions, he is still, morally, as much in bondage to his instincts as an animal, and can, therefore, fall victim at any moment to the beast within.*
>
> C. G. JUNG

Despite these shocking truths, I continued to contemplate. I could see how it was the masculine part of us that drove us to experiment in this way. With its insatiable hunger to know and its thirst to expand, it used its brilliance of mind to reach its zenith with the splitting of the atom. Unfortunately, it was this level of experimentation that led man into the realm of the gods, that gave him access to powers that he was not ready for or responsible enough to handle. Some say this should never have happened, and yet it did.

Therefore, there is a reason, and it's up to us to figure out why.

David Krieger, president of the Nuclear Age Peace Foundation, notes,

> We in the technologically advanced West were therefore unable to recognize that splitting the atom in 1945 was an act of sacrilege against a Sacred Order; that using the elements of life to destroy life would lead to unforeseen consequences that would be beyond our power to control. In the nuclear bomb, we have created a weapon that is not only amoral, but truly demonic. We thought we could control the power we had unleashed but since our actions have a shadow aspect of which we are unaware, this comes back to face us in the situation of extreme danger we face today as the US and North Korea confront each other, both led by men who are morally ill-equipped to carry such an immense responsibility.*

You may be wondering why I'm using this subject matter for the "She Who Knows" chapter, and why I'm using the discovery of nuclear power as a cry for the vast and full awakening of our intuition. Well, if it was the masculine part of us that reached its zenith with the splitting of the atom, then it only stands to reason that the feminine part of us must also reach her zenith point too, in a way that not only balances this godlike power but also knows what to do with it.

I cannot help but feel that the vast and unprecedented growth

---

*David Krieger, "10 Lessons You Should Learn about Nuclear Weapons," March 1, 2019, Nuclear Weapons: An Absolute Evil, Anne Baring's website.

surge of the feminine that must come if we are to responsibly handle these powers will arise from the deepest wells of wisdom and intuition and result in an equally impressive discovery. I personally feel that the feminine will discover a power within Her that balances this discovery in a way we have not yet imagined. This could of course mean the total destruction of it. Or there's the possibility that the feminine will create a field that responsibly holds this power in check, preventing any harm and devastation. And because of Her ability to reach for these previously unused abilities, this feminine field of "holding" a Divine power creates a birthing bed of yet unknown pro-life discoveries.

What we do know, or perhaps sense, is how this kind of discovery within the feminine will lead us to the genuine qualities of She Who Knows, and the embodiment of Her. It is only by this level of being that a truly Divine avatar can naturally and unassumingly take on human form. Possibly because that is precisely what now needs to happen. We can't get rid of nuclear power. It's already here, and even if we were to turn off the generators and attempt to destroy all the weapons we would still have a volatile substance on our hands that simply doesn't go away.

As the world is in peril and our continued existence is in question, the feminine must urgently discover something about herself that is of the same magnitude as nuclear power, as it is the only thing that can balance the off-limits discovery made all those years ago.

Could the full awakening of the Fierce Feminine responsibly balance out what the masculine part of us has already created? Could we undo what has already been done? My answer is this: Undo? No. Evolve through? Yes.

Whenever I contemplate the journey of awakening and living within the fully illumined and embodied feminine principle, I can't help sensing how the fruits of this grace will spill over to every aspect of life. I've been using the word *discovery,* but that's not it. It feels more like permission. And how this potential ability that we are seeking is so very close. It feels like it is within our own breath. It is most definitely within reach, and we do not have to earn the right to discover it or prove ourselves worthy in any way. All of this kind of thinking is a masculine way of looking at things. If we know anything about the feminine, it's about surrender and letting go of all the motivators and drives. By allowing something to come through us—not by force or sheer will, but by being. This could be the "permission" and key that opens up a new world.

If there's one thing we can be mindful of right now it's the endless tendency to be busy with distractions and the inner chaos in our own hearts and minds. This again is an incredibly masculine state of being. It would be wise for us, as the feminine principle, to spend equally as much time in an open and receptive quality of mind and lifestyle to match. This would at least give us the opportunity to slow down, rest, and encounter a part of us that has been purposely kept out of reach.

It is the feminine part of us that streams wisdom into our awareness, guides us toward love, softens us into forgiveness, and blesses us with grace. Without the feminine, we cannot receive. It is truly that simple. We will only carry on working and toiling with sweat upon our brows for something we will never get because it's out of reach. The feminine puts that which was once out of reach within our hands. She bestows upon us trust, wisdom, compassion, and mercy.

We must develop the feminine part of our consciousness and adopt a lifestyle that supports this. By developing the feminine part of the brain, we will have access to wisdom and intuition. Instead of thinking, we will learn to reflect, contemplate, expand upon, and then be able to reveal. All these qualities greatly strengthen our ability to discern, feel into, know the truth of, and thereby protect and sustain our Light and essence. This is the problem with the human mind; the feminine principle is missing. It is not being accessed. Therefore, the mind as it currently is cannot make rational decisions, because half of it is not being consulted and taken into consideration.

PRACTICES FOR OPENING
TO THE FEMININE PRINCIPLE

In the sections below I describe some key practices that I have picked up over the years that have opened me to the feminine stream of consciousness and its value in day-to-day functionality. This part of my journey has been priceless, as it has also led to direct revelation and an on-going relationship with indescribable gnosis.

Return to Darkness

Darkness is a place of transformation. Darkness is a place of restoration. Darkness is a place of profound healing. Darkness is a place of sanctuary and quiet refuge from the overwhelming intensity of day-to-day living. I often wonder whether we have forgotten this parallel world and the restorative medicine it offers us. It seems as if we want to avoid darkness at every cost. As soon as it naturally comes, on come the lights. Instead, we could relish the seeping blackness as we lie back and surrender into its velvet no-thingness and reflect upon its silent embrace. Instead, we often see it as inconvenient and a time of enforced rest, rather than the mystical entrance into the otherworld that it truly is.

When we consciously enter darkness and commune with it as a living substance rather than the absence of light, we will realize that it is teeming with an otherworldly presence. This presence, in my experience, soothes and settles our jittery, overstimulated nervous system by dropping it down a few notches into a theta wave, an oscillating frequency of deep, harmonious healing. Every form of artificial debris that surrounds us (Wi-Fi, computers, cell phones, etc.) evaporates in darkness. We become stripped of all the unseen and invisible artificial intelligence (AI) networks that move in and around us against our will. In the natural darkness, we encounter a time and place that is devoid of AI and its partnering with the Dark Agenda. And this is critically important. Because here, in this place, we can find our true Self, once the fears and phobias settle down. Here is where we find our true origins and original blueprint.

My husband and I are blessed to be living in the French Pyrenees with their numerous limestone caves that once sheltered our prehistoric ancestors and provided an initiatory passageway from one world to the next. Within an hour's drive are the Cathar initiation caves, which always guarantee a direct one-to-one meeting with the primordial wisdom that dwells there. These potent caves of transformation offer us a place to reflect, to see, and to know. They have been used for centuries by esoteric groups, and the moment you step into them you realize why: they're teaming with a thick, palpable, and indwelling living presence that draws you close, surrounds you, and then eventually penetrates all that you are.

All external references are gone. The appearance of your body is gone. The space in which you are sitting is gone. Everything turns in to meet the inner world, and that, of course, can be frightening *and* exciting.

I think the first thing we must realize is that darkness isn't only empty space. In certain places, like the caves of initiation I mentioned above, it's alive. It emerges to take you on a journey of deep reflection and insight. It takes you to the place inside where you will meet She Who Knows—the seat of intuition.

As to be expected, the Dark Agenda is busy with a whole variety of distractions to make sure we don't have the time or energy to spend in this revelatory space. And to top it off, from an early age, the Dark Agenda sets into motion a program that makes us afraid of the dark, branding it as something to avoid at all costs. Those monsters we were afraid of, those ghouls under the bed, those ghosts in the attic are simply the Dark Agenda program.

Darkness, beloved friends, is where we find the Self. And what better way to distract us from going there than by making us afraid of the dark.

To say that all light is good is as if you said that all water is good—or even that all clear or transparent water is good; it would not be true. One must see what is the nature of the light or where it comes from or what is in it before one can say that it is the true Light. False lights

*exist and misleading lustres, lower lights too that belong to
the being's inferior reaches. One must therefore be on one's
guard and distinguish; the true discrimination has to come
by growth of the psychic feeling and a purified mind and
experience.*

SRI AUROBINDO, *BASES OF YOGA*

Even if you don't have access to natural darkness, like caves or
places of low-level light pollution, you can still create a darkness experience in your own home. First, you need to find a room in your house
that is already naturally dark, and ideally, close to a bathroom. Then,
you start to make it even darker, by blocking out all the light. You
can drape heavy materials at the windows, seal off any shafts of light
under the doors, and even select a blindfold to wear. Make sure you
have a comfortable place to sleep and some floor space for yoga or
some form of stretching. Prepare a plentiful supply of spring water
and simple-to-digest natural foods. When you're in the dark your
sense of appetite diminishes; you don't really get hungry, although you
do get thirsty. Even when you take a shower, or use the toilet, you are
still in the dark.

An ideal amount of time would be a two-and-a-half-day period.
This could begin at sundown on a Friday and finish at sunrise on a
Monday. During this time, simply allow yourself to sit in meditation,
rest, sleep, chant, pray, and stretch as you slowly become consumed by
darkness. There is no reading or writing (obviously). This time in the
dark will allow you to foster positive and enlightening associations
with darkness.

Many people who practice darkness retreats feel that the dark contains a lot of energy. It reminds them of the womb, the source of life. In
many religious and spiritual traditions, darkness is thought to lie under
all creation. Everything else is added to darkness. It can be helpful when
meditating to think of darkness as a base from which our reflection and
further insight can emerge.

Heaven's Tea

I first came across Heaven's Tea School of Sacred Tea Arts a few years ago when I was staying at OneDoorLand community in Portland, Oregon. It was here that I met Tea Monk Po. He brought me into his temple, which was more like a library. His teas were wrapped in brown paper bags and sealed with strange and ancient markings. I felt I was in the coliseum of tea medicine.

He explained that the tea I was about to drink had come from pure land and sacred mountains. He told me to listen deeply and smell the lifting aroma of the natural elixir. He explained that each tea is a particular energy and plant spirit, and that these spirits are constantly talking to us, if we only have the ears to listen.

He invited me to pray and open to the experience . . .

I remember the smell. It was ancient, of the earth, dependable and anchored. I knew I could trust this. I invited in the spirit, which reminded me of the local enchanted fairy forests near our home. I inwardly saw my red blood become emerald green as the tree spirit began to take over. Yes, I wanted this. I was more than happy to become both plant and human. Even just the idea of this relaxed me. The awkwardness of my humanity fell away, as my true face was revealed. Tears of beauty revealed and tender gratitude fell from my face, as I tasted the earth and the simplicity of the moment.

I became my real Self. And that real Self knew all. In that revelatory and fully present moment I realized that this tea was a gateway to the medicine of the natural world in a swift and beautiful-to-consume tincture. In this subtle, yogic state, I forgave myself for being human—only because the tea wanted me to, only because the tea needed me to.

In hindsight, I can truly say that I experienced a visceral realization of my humanity and Divinity and how to move through this life embracing both as sacred. It was like a liquid, open-eyed, fully grounded mystical experience. My body totally relaxed, my mind became silent, and everything was simple and easy. Heaven's Tea School of Sacred Tea Arts is gentle, subtle, and graceful. I have not experienced ayahuasca or any other plant medicines, so I cannot speak to their effects, but from what I have heard, they're nothing like the cathartic experience I had with this tea.

The spirit within these teas is gentle, delicate, tender, and playful. These teas rejuvenate, restore, heal, and revitalize the system. They are a true gift from the Creator to heal human beings.

Voice in the Wilderness

The last practice I wish to share with you is walking in nature. Prolonged walking in nature. We have all been for a walk, but have you gone for a seven-hour walk? Have you allowed yourself to get lost, get wet, go above the tree line, and speak to no one for the whole day? This great gift was revealed to me by my husband. He is a keen walker and has done it most of his life. I, on the other hand, had only walked for a couple of hours at a time, and so this was a new adventure.

I advise you to treat the experience as a shamanic interaction with the natural world. Placing it honorably alongside the darkness retreat and Heaven's Tea as a powerful tool to install She Who Knows. This is where She lives. Like the caves, this is where She is most potent. But it takes a bit more time for Her to start getting under your skin and rearranging things into their rightful order. I have no idea why; it simply does.

When my husband took me above the tree line, up into the higher altitudes of the French Pyrenees, I glimpsed heaven on Earth. I felt peace and could witness the harmony of nature and my own place in it. I saw perfection. I felt the simplicity of what it could be like to be this new human on the Earth. I glimpsed a world free from the oppression of the mind. The natural world victoriously freed my mind, after quite a few hours of complaining and imagining, "I just can't do it." But I could, and so can you. Because we must.

I often use our longer three-day walks as a vision quest. A vision quest can be understood as an essential rite of passage that can mark a significant life transition or change. It can also be used as a time and space to find answers, not by thinking or planning but rather by allowing something else, beyond our minds, to be revealed by the natural world. And reveal She does!

There is a great line by the poet David Whyte that says, "The forest knows where you are. You must let it find you." And that is exactly it. We must allow ourselves to be found, and usually, fortunately or unfortunately, that requires an initiation, a catalyzing event that changes everything—right there on the spot.

And so when you make that great prayer to be taken on a vision quest, you will come back with answers. And the One who gave them to you will be watching for your promised action, and if that doesn't come . . . Well, honestly, we may not be given another chance.

There are key elements that make up an authentic vision quest. This includes time alone, a natural place (solitude), fasting (emptiness), exposure to the elements (vulnerability), and self-reliance (self-trust). Researchers are increasingly recognizing that direct and immediate contact with the natural world promotes health and development and that a disconnection from the natural world has negative consequences for human health and development. The documented benefits of spending time in nature include stress reduction, fascination with and appreciation for the environment, a sense of competence and self-esteem balanced with a sense of trust in oneself and the world, a more mature morality and care for others, and a sense of awe, wonder, and sacredness. Direct contact with nature also leads to a greater commitment to positive environmental action.

We live in a world marked by borders; borders between continents, people, and even between our own hearts and minds. And perhaps one of the most pervasive borders is the one we've mistakenly placed between ourselves and nature. It is a complete lie that humans are not a part of nature. The truth is, we *are* nature!

I close with this quote from the beloved, late Steven Foster, who founded the School of Lost Borders along with his wife Meredith Little.

My Soul is striving to remember who I am, to make who I am compatible with who I was born to be, to bring who I am into synch with who I will be.

STEVEN FOSTER

So as this chapter ends, I truly advise you to seek out the transformational powers that lie hidden in darkness, solitude, and nature's offerings. For most of us, the natural world is a disappearing place. And perhaps now you know the reason why. It places within our hands a first-class ticket to authentically being able to live in harmony as our true Self upon this Earth.

However, there is something astonishing I would like to share with you. I used to live in the heart of London and was often consumed by all the recognizable stresses and strains of urban living. But somewhere along the path, I made a series of small and frightening decisions that led me to the French Pyrenees. And I could never remain here if I still believed in the empty promises and numerous sacrifices required for the locked and loaded mind invested in false idols and the world of privilege and entitlement.

I have this feeling that as we continue our path, as our mind becomes freer, clearer, and a truer reflection of our uncomplicated essence, we find ourselves starting to make decisions—about where we live, how we live, and what we partake in, as we live. As we unhook from the Dark Agenda, its influence over us begins to wane and diminish, and all the things we were once addicted to cease to be important anymore. Fame, success, money, and copious amounts of sex all dwindle, slipping through our fingers as we laugh hysterically at our own letting go. We stagger backward as the light bathes our faces, wiping away the years of brutal separation—man and God, nature and concrete, and money and seeds.

As we retrieve our own wisdom and learn to trust it, I expect we will seek out the inner and outer environments that nourish it. This requires faith and trust, stepping out of our comfort zones and embracing the unknown and unpredictable. The "counterarguments" for this process are the voices of the Dark Agenda coming through the ego, reinforced by the program that worships personality over essence. It doesn't like to give up its reign, for it would mean the end of its rule. These thought injections are not stemming from the true Self but from the impersonation of ourselves.

We come to know that any difficulties and challenging situations that may arise are opportunities for a deeper awakening, most often resulting in "shocks" that are necessary to shake us up and yank us out of illusion. Despite these moments of fierce grace, we also experience more and more beautiful equanimity and moments of bliss, happiness, and joy that don't depend on any external factors.

We become less afraid of discomfort and the unknown, realizing on a much subtler level that life is not about "winning" or "losing" but is a series of lessons. We realize that we are being guided and helped at every moment if only we remember to tune in to our own magnificence. As we do this, we become more in touch with our intuition and our internal wisdom, connected essentially with Divine will, all of which are uniquely expressed through us as sovereign, embodied, Soul-integrated individuals. Life then becomes more effortless, as we don't try to fight the current of life but trust that the river of life carries us where we need to be and inspires us to become something far wilder, far more natural, and far more innocent.

And so, as we come full circle in this chapter, we remember—it's two minutes to midnight, and the feminine must urgently discover something about Herself that is of the same magnitude as nuclear power, as it is only this that can and will balance the off-limits discovery made all those years ago. Freed from insidious mutterings of the Dark Agenda, She will not only find it but beautifully and gloriously become it.

Thousands of tired, nerve-shaken, over-civilized people are beginning to find out that going to the mountains is going home; that wildness is a necessity.

JOHN MUIR

Transmission
Darkening of the Light*

Come into a comfortable lying-down position with your feet flopped open, your palms face up, and your eyes closed, as you start to draw every part of yourself into the inner, into the Self, the genuine Self. Breath after breath you make that journey, meeting the energy that you feel inside of you, the part of you that prays with earnest devotion. Breath after breath, you fill that place up, becoming more and more true, as you lie here settling in as the one who has said yes to show up for this transmission. As you start to settle, the mind becomes still—open, honest—your heart becomes palpable, filled with feeling and availability. Your body is settled, resting on the bed or the floor, the tension is easing out of your muscles, and your joints are relaxing. Your bones are dropping further into your skin.

A beautiful wave of rest floods your body, giving the signal to the nerves and the glands to settle into a deeper theta wave. The masculine part of you weds the feminine part of you, thereby creating the Sacred One. The human part of you weds the Divine part of you, thereby creating the Sacred One, with its absolute union with life, with creation, with its sacred origins before human life is chosen.

You begin this transmission drawing on your sacred origins. You are coming from that place, breathing from that place, your love is being revealed because of that place. You begin to feel a warm glow from your heart space, and it is the genuine love of the Divine. It is the father love, it is the mother love, it is agape, it is worship, it is devotion, compassion, and mercy. When you start to feel that warmth in your chest, that is when you find yourself making your way to your front door. But before you open that front door, you will step out and into one of the destruction stories that breaks your heart. We've all heard them; that's why you're here. You're going to step out

---

*An audio track of this meditative exercise can be downloaded at audio.innertraditions .com/fiferi.

and into the one that hurts the most. You're going to step out on behalf of humankind, animal kind, nature, the elements, and all the things we cannot name but only feel. So, when you're ready, let's begin this work.

See yourself holding the door handle of your front door, as you step out and into an extinction scene that you have already imagined. As you step out into this world, you are being tasked only to walk through it slowly, with tremendous presence, witnessing it with a soft, warm heart. You are walking out and into this world where all the familiar buildings that made up your neighborhood are now gone; only rubble is left behind. You cannot define what was once buildings, what was cars, what was schools, what was roads. Everything is charred and blackened, pulverized, and broken.

And as you walk over this rubble with your bare feet, you are breathing, and you are being intimate with your surroundings. You're not looking for bodies, because no one and no thing has survived. Use your inner eyes and your inner ears to navigate through this scene. The air is thick and dirty. Pieces of debris fill the air and land on your face and your lips—perhaps these are ashes from people, animals, trees . . . You are truly with all of this, bringing human consciousness to the scene. This has happened many times before. Or maybe this is the first time. Can you be present with this possible reality? Every now and again you recognize something, in its blackened, scorched form. Yet nothing is left. You begin praying in a language of your Soul, uttering sounds that clean, and clean, and clean—and do what is needed in the moment. You simply respond.

All the fish are dead in the waters. All the birds have fallen from the sky. The last lions have roared. There are no more animals; we have killed them along with ourselves. The elemental energies are confused and are becoming a new element. There is chaos, but it is ordered. Continue walking through the scene, seeing it all, bearing it all, witnessing it all.

Man has reached his zenith. We have annihilated the world. Killed every last one of us. Dragged nature with us. The sun is dark, the mountains are smoking. The waters are black. From your sacred origins, the language known and unknown begins to pass through your lips. You are speaking the language of angels as they tread upon our ruins. Words being spoken.

Words saved for this moment. As you continue, you start to get glimpses of the other continents. You start to see our classical monuments have been pulverized and shattered. The great temples of India, the pyramids of Egypt, the monuments of Rome and Greece, the Great Wall of China, Stonehenge, Newgrange, Easter Island—all gone. No record, no evidence, no keepsake of our existence. We have been taken away. We have been made extinct. Beloved one, please be brave to feel as deeply as you can feel. To feel our whole species extinct.

The mind is open, the heart is available. Be here to witness the darkening of the Light.

The heart is warm, that flame is still burning. As you continue to walk, you notice tiny, delicate, little green shoots beginning to show their tender faces through the rubble, through the destruction, slowly, slowly, slowly. A little bit of nature hopes, dares to be born. Nature is beginning to take in and recycle our destruction. Growing over the top of our great mistakes comes the beginning of a new cycle.

When you have seen enough, come to your knees on a chosen piece of land that once meant the world to you. As you come to your knees in an act of prayer, as the last one, the last human—you show your face to the Beloved One, owning what our race has done. You show your face, you show your eyes, you show your heart. You open your arms, and you cry out to the world, to the Beloved One, and its angels, "I am the last!"

All around you is carnage, but also the first green shoots of hope. When you are ready, bring that beautiful golden chest of yours to the earth in full prostration, as you yourself get taken, pulverized into dust. Right before that happens, your golden heart kisses the earth in absolute pardon and apology. Leaving your last words to nature, as each and every single one of us gets extinguished like candles all around the world, on behalf of balance, harmony, and prayer.

May the grace of the holy Sophia be with us, always.

※·※

Acts of Evil

A terrorist is any person who uses unlawful violence and relentless intimidation to weaken or kill.

Since writing the thirteen Sorrows of the World, I have come to realize that humanity is inflicting the most horrendous acts of terror on the natural world. Not only are we all capable of doing this, but there are some of us who relish the opportunity to inflict pain and suffering on another. This is an act of evil.

I have heard firsthand stories of farm and abattoir workers stabbing defenseless Friesian cows who are in line to be killed, kicking over-milked dairy cows who are too exhausted to stand up, and bludgeoning piglets, just because. I have seen footage of people using a blowtorch inside a dog's mouth to prepare it for the Yulin Dog Meat Festival. I

213

know of people who beat up, torture, and sometimes even kill their animals, because of their own frustrations.

These are all acts of evil.

> *The question is not "can they [animals] reason?" or "can they talk?" but "can they suffer?"*
>
> JEREMY BENTHAM

Animals are the same as us. They seek comfort, they seek safety, and they seek a life free from pain. It's moralistically wrong to breed any type of sentient life for the sole reason of feeding us. This is as morally and humanly wrong as nuclear weapons. This is as wrong as domestic violence. This is as wrong as stoning a woman to death. This is as wrong as electric shock treatment for people suffering from mental dis-ease.

When the full force of the feminine awakens within us there will be no more factory farms. If people wish to continue to eat meat and dairy, they will know in their hearts that they must hand care for and nurture these animals on their own land and ask permission for the gifts they may offer. The animals will be treated with the utmost compassion and kindness, and if slaughter must come, it is to be done in a dignified and honorable way, with reverent acknowledgment of their sacrifice.

But it doesn't stop there.

Inexplicable acts are also happening in interrogation centers across the world. We inflict immeasurable bodily harm and physiological warfare on anyone who is a prisoner of war or even suspected to be some kind of serious threat to the state. This is an act of evil.

On and on down the rabbit hole we go—pedophilia, world-wide corruption, ritual abuse . . . This brutality must be stopped altogether. I believe there should be a new kind of human being in the making, that this strain of evil needs to be purified from our being. I also believe we need to be proactive with this healing and pray, no beg, for this wickedness to be lifted from within us and around us. Until I performed the research for this book, I didn't know what was truly going on in the meat and dairy industries. I didn't know anything about the Yulin Dog Meat Festival or canned hunting. I never dared to research the *Stoning of Soraya M.* But now that I have, I can clearly see what must change. Within our codex is a loveless gene. A barren, unfeeling, and uncaring strain of wickedness and cruelty. A cold and isolated and sometimes arrogant, or perhaps unworthy, voice. The New Age says this is the ego. I am not so sure how true that is anymore.

Looking with the eyes of gnosis, we would say this is the part of us that contains the seed of anti-awakening. Perhaps within us, there is a homing beacon that can hear, sense, and receive the broadcast from the Dark Agenda—that's how it gets in; that's how the game continues to be played. But what if we turned that frequency off? What would that look like? What if we could locate where within us this seed lies hidden, and hold it to the Light, not to change it, but to simply expose it to a source that can penetrate, irrigate, and suffuse it with Light?

This kind of inner contemplation reminds me of the understanding that there are three kinds of human being: one who has no interest in the Light and never will, one who seeks earnestly to become a better person and does seek out the Light, and a third who is made of the Light and can be nothing other than that. I suspect many of us would like to believe we are of the third type, but that is doubtful. I imagine we are more of the second kind, seeking the Light earnestly but with no guarantee that the Light we are absorbing is the True Light.

We are in a time of the false Light, and there is no better time than now to go the extra mile in our journey of awakening. Find the place within that picks up on the force of anti-awakening and listens and believes its message to be true, and then, in that almost kidnapped place, show it to the holiest Light you can reach for, and say, "I am sovereign. I am free and I chose this!"

Expose your inner terrorist—an inner presence who uses unlawful violence and relentless intimidation to weaken or kill—to the Light and see what occurs.

This is an act of grace.

Pause here for reflection. Take the time that is needed to truly be with these insights and understandings. Just breathe and be with them. Let's bear witness to the sobriety of the situation and feel one another as we rise together to receive more of Her transmission.

Let's move on without answers.

We must learn to trust the process, remembering that *this is an initiation*.

THIRTEEN
Original Innocence

THE ROLE OF THIS THIRTEENTH CHAPTER is to emanate the entirety of this transmission from the Fierce Feminine and the many veils of reality She has lifted from us. We may be feeling obliterated, hopeless, and overwhelmed with this new information as we begin to see and come to terms with a deeper reality within and around us. But this will pass. Because it *has* to.

And this is why I have titled this chapter "Original Innocence." Because I believe we knew this before we agreed—and maybe even nominated ourselves—to come here. We knew the enormity of what we were saying yes to, but we did not take into account the almost complete loss of identity and remembrance of where we came from and what we're capable of achieving.

Like the holy Sophia, who purposefully relinquished Her Divinity to fall to Earth in order to bring the Light of wisdom, we did not bank on what was waiting for us. We had no clue about the enormous and widespread insidious sludge of Archonic influence that infiltrates the whole of society, including the endless attempts to penetrate our own minds. Under its sedation we could not imagine the everyday horrors revealed in the "Sorrows of the World," or that the Dark Agenda was real and fully operative in our governments, law courts, and police forces or our health, pharmaceutical, food, sex, arms, drug, educational, and peace-keeping industries.

It is everywhere. Inside and outside of us. It is an invasive energy designed to twist, misrepresent, and turn upside down and inside out. It is a trickster in a hall of mirrors. But its power is absolutely limited. In order for the Dark Agenda to continue to reign over us, it requires our compliance, gleaned from our ignorance, apathy, and cowardice.

The last "Sorrow of the World," appearing at the end of this chapter, is titled, "Why Did You Do It? Why Did You Let Me?" because I believe this is precisely the answer: those of us who are not currently being used as agents for the Dark Agenda (because it really is a moment-by-moment choice!) simply have to rise up and be active with our wakefulness and bust past the conditioning that says, "It's not okay to interfere, to say no, to challenge authority, to have a difference of opinion, or to go it alone." Because, beloved friends, it is most certainly okay to do all of those things. And do them we must.

We have unlimited access to the Light if only we turn to face it. The problem is, we have been brainwashed into thinking we are facing the Light, but realistically it's probably the false light drip-fed to us by the Dark Agenda. False light is glamourous and self-serving. It brings us acknowledgment, recognition, affirmation, and all kinds of other addictive, greedy goo. It makes us feel important and powerful.

The true Light, on the other hand, often makes us cry. It's that simple. The moment we come into contact with it, our humility emerges and we take a breath of fresh, clean air. It's a gorgeous moment. Our sense of individuality is gone! The Self is united. End of story. All is well.

When we turn to face the Light, for real, that's when we will not only see the change but also be working alongside others to produce it. I used to think the ancient spiritual and religious traditions represented a heavy and straight path, one that was way too serious and time-consuming for me to take on. But now I feel different. Now I'm beginning to really understand the gravitas of the situation and the enormous efforts we have to make. But instead of seeing this as a gloomy, heavy-hearted trudge toward a faraway horizon, I feel strangely uplifted. I feel optimistic because I know without a shadow of a doubt

She is here for us now. I also feel you. I can feel your heart and Soul drinking this nectar up, and I can also feel you, feeling me.

We are awakening, and we will awaken more. Our innocence knows who we are, where we came from, and where we are going. And God knows we need to remember, and fast. We can. And we will.

As Bernhard Guenther noted in a Facebook post:

This loneliness we experience and inability to "fit in" anywhere has its purpose (including the suffering we experience) and if we keep on the track with faith and trust, learning our lessons with sincerity, patience, humility and courage, it will lead us to true love, real companionship and a conscious connection with Spirit/Source as we find our way "back home" reuniting with the Divine. We start to experience magical positive synchronicities and help/support of the Divine Force that responds to our call and supports and guides us in unexpected ways. Doors open where there have been no doors before. Out of the dark, we emerge into the Light. The only way out is through and we realize (embodied, not merely philosophically or intellectually) that we were never alone but under a spell of separation from all that IS.

Now that I, too, have come to this place, and I'm sitting right alongside you, I find myself reflecting on the enormous journey I have been on. This book has been nine months in the making and ended on one of the most powerful lunar eclipses of our time. I have trusted Her methods every step of the way despite, at times, having a real struggle on my hands. I had to let go—often. I had to hand over my being to Her charge. My mind fretted that I wasn't "doing enough" and that there would be 101 reasons why this book wouldn't be published. Luckily, I was able walk and walk and walk in the mountains, and She would fill me with Herself. I did not realize it at the time, but I was on an energetic detox. She inspired me to write with pen and paper, in little bits and often, rather than sitting for hours at a time on the computer.

Often, I would have no idea how to begin a chapter, and then within days a real-life situation would emerge that gave me precisely what I needed to be able to write from an authentic place.

She asked me to write the words out, rather than type them. It was astonishing to see a very different voice appear on the page from this practice. It was a game changer for me, and this is how She asks us to work—so that we may absolutely trust Her promptings. We must do it by leaving our mind at the door and making the change(s) we're being guided to. This was one of many radical realizations I had since allowing this Divine presence into my life. I can honestly say these past nine months have turned out to be one of the most direct and potent growth spurts I have ever experienced. There is no doubt I have been orchestrated and governed by a persistent, initiatory, and incomprehensibly wise force. This journey with the Fierce Feminine has delivered precisely what She said it would—a template of awakening and an antidote for the venomous sedation of the Dark Agenda.

Now that I have received this, there is no going back. Too much has happened, too much has been seen, and way too much has been said.

When I first started to welcome in this energy I imagined that the end result would be some kind of embodied warrior-queen priestess, who was clearly empowered, fierce, outspoken, and forthcoming. Now that I am writing out this final chapter, I realize that's not it at all. When the title "Original Innocence" emerged from within me, I was confused because it came with a palpable energy, and an insistence to be felt. There was a clarity to it, a cleanness and a quiet sovereignty. It was like a breath of fresh air or like standing before a presence that genuinely loves you. This presence was empty of clutter, and I knew it was holiness. It was mercy.

This template is an act of mercy.

That word always brings me to tears because I feel what it means and I see what it offers, and that cannot be written, only felt.

I realize now how this process has been an act of mercy. Together, we have stripped away the many masks of vanity, compromise, entitlement, protection, conditioning, and cheapening of our own dignity and knowing. I am no longer partaking in any form of prostitution. I stand as I am—in original innocence. Unmasked and awake.

There is one more point I would like to make before I disappear into the mist. At the beginning of this journey, I had a sense of myself and a sense of Her. As you may have noticed, I capitalized *Her* and *She* as a reference to the Fierce Feminine. Now that this transmission has been completed, I humbly recognize how Her presence is now part of me. I remember the day when I stood on that Templar ground, tentatively calling in the presence of Kali and being afraid of what that might look like and where that might lead. Never in my wildest dreams could I have imagined something like this was possible, that She has become a welcomed and integrated part of Me. Or I, Her.

I guess what I'm trying to say in all of this is how effortless the journey actually was and is. The hurdles are in our minds. Even when massive challenges arise in grounded reality, the hurdle is in our minds. We are capable of everything. Take one step toward Her, and She will take ten toward you.

After all these years, it's clear to me that there are three paths that can lead to a genuine Spiritual Awakening: the first is by the grace of a wise teacher, rooted in their connection to primal Source; the second is by the chiseling and refinement found within a group of soulfully mature people; and the third, and perhaps most rapid, is by a spontaneous catalyst delivered by life itself.

I feel we are in the time of the third option. We have come as far as we can with wise teachers, and our peers have shared the very best of themselves. And yet we know there are still pockets of dishonor and denial that require Her special kind of shakeups that come only in times like these. What I have noticed about these spontaneous awakenings is that they occur when we least expect it. They seem to appear out of the blue, as we are relaxing in our skin or feel we're on a roll with something. Then, boom! With the element of surprise, She appears in our lives with an important and timely message.

I believe some of us are fast approaching the frontier of spontaneous awakening. We are being edged and herded toward a great epiphany of change. We know we can't continue living the way we have been. There is no growth or awakening without first seeing and acknowledging our existing disappointments, and how we have dishonored, and perhaps continue to dishonor, the gift of life in every possible way.

Acknowledging our disappointments and the way we destroy almost everything means becoming aware of the deeply held sense of "lostness" that we all carry. It means becoming aware that something is desperately missing from our lives. Covering up these feelings leads to the almost impenetrable rings of guilt, shame, and remorse that keep out our truly wise teachers and the inspiring encouragement of well-meaning counsel. Only we, or perhaps She, will have exactly what it takes to get past our defenses, which were employed for good reason, but are now in the way and must be relinquished for genuine awakening to occur.

In times like these, it would be wise to pray deeply, meditate daily, and stay in regular connection with our friends and animal companions. Be out in nature and with God and realize that no matter how terrifying the situation is, it is perhaps an ordained situation with the fundamental purpose to make us finally do the work to realize who we really are, and to act accordingly.

> *Sorrow prepares you for joy. It violently sweeps everything out of your house, so that new joy can find space to enter. It shakes the yellow leaves from the bough of your heart, so that fresh, green leaves can grow in their place. It pulls up the rotten roots, so that new roots hidden beneath have room to grow. Whatever sorrow shakes from your heart, far better things will take their place.*
>
> RUMI

I am so used to reaching the end of a book and offering some kind of conclusion. But this time, there isn't one.

We have received Her template for awakening. She has revealed the nature of the many influences that surround us, preventing our species from realizing its Divinity and making creative choices from that awake place. She has also spoken of the numerous ways we have remained silent and compliant with this force, and the price we and all of nature will pay if we allow this to carry on.

Let us give ourselves the time and space needed to reflect upon what we have read, what we have felt, and who we have become while doing it.

And as they say in this part of the world—

May peace be with you.

Transmission

The Original Rape*

Come into a comfortable lying-down or seated position, with your eyes closed and looking down into the blackness of your warm existence on the inside. Become aware of your breathing. Witness the inhale and the exhale. Then bring them into balance. Shape them so they become mirror images of one another. Deep, fluid breaths. Use this time to drop the body, to drop the brain, and spread yourself out on the inside, so you become a feeling horizon of unobstructed possibility and potential for unimaginable healings, insights, and retrievals of once exiled fragments of yourself, or your Self.

Use this time to become vast, open, and allowing. Start to take yourself back to the time of the Temple, those ancient days of the Temple, as opposed to the Church. It doesn't matter where you are, what epoch you are in—the stories, the civilization, and the period don't matter. Just take yourself back to the vibrational texture of the Temple.

Your Soul will guide you.

---

*An audio track of this meditative exercise can be downloaded at audio.innertraditions .com/fiferi.

Your Soul will start to invoke the imagery, the sensations, and the memories of the time that you have chosen to do this work in.

Once upon a time in the days of the Temple, there was a group of priests who were led by a High Priest, and there was a group of priestesses who were led by a High Priestess. These men and women were the spiritual patriarchs and matriarchs of their people, their land, and their lifestyle. This lineage of priests and priestesses flowed from the father to the son and from the mother to the daughter, respectively. This was a lineage and a legacy passed down through the generations.

The priestesses took care of everything that was embodied and part of the creation. They oversaw the crops, the merriment, the beauty, the healing, the medicine, the childbirth, and the rites of passage of their people. And they did this with great care, great integrity, and great love.

The priests took care of the cosmic aspect of the Creator. The Light, the guidance, the intelligence, the direction, and the orchestration of their spiritual work.

And together they would meet in the Temple to perform their sacred union work for the betterment of their people, to glorify God, and to bring a benevolent wave of goodness to all of existence.

A specific ritual was held every year where a young maiden was birthed into the priestess line. A virgin came into the Temple space to be initiated and receive the All, the Absolute, and the Only in a sacred sexual initiation.

This young maiden was guided and primed and readied by the priestesses who had passed through this initiation already. She was taken to the altar in all of her purity, in all of her wonderment, as the priests and priestesses invoked the Almighty Spirit to come into the Temple, and to come into this young maiden so she may be initiated into receiving and conceiving the fullness of the Light. Penetrated by Almighty God deep into her heart, womb, and Soul so that she may conceive and birth out into this world the continuation of the lineage and the strengthening of the legacy. This work had been going on for centuries.

On this day, the High Priestess leads this maiden into the Temple. The priestesses guide the maiden to the altar, which is decorated with fresh flowers, herbs, sheepskins, and silks. The entire Temple is perfumed with frankincense, myrrh, and powerful oils to invoke a deep spiritual state of consciousness.

The young maiden lies in wait on the altar wearing a sheer dress, inwardly reciting her prayers, trembling with anticipation, sinking down deep into her faith and knowingness that she was in the right place, at the right time.

The priests then walk into the Temple and the atmosphere becomes electric, with a distinct charge filling the air. The High Priest walks over to the High Priestess, asking to speak to her discreetly. He takes her to one side, out of earshot of everyone else. He solemnly explains to her that he has been given the instruction from the All, the Absolute, and the Only that on this day it is the priests who shall be holding the space in the Temple for God to descend into this young maiden, and that the priestesses and the High Priestess needed to be outside of the Temple as they do their work to hold the space.

Profound silence is born between them.

The High Priestess listens carefully on the inside. She has always trusted her dear friend. This work has been going on for centuries—she trusts him—and yet, this has never happened before. The High Priestess inwardly searches for wisdom. The time is passing, and the moment is now.

She feels torn. She searches the face of the High Priest, and he is looking at her solemnly, witnessing her turmoil, imploring her to reach for the answer in time for the ritual to begin.

No true answer comes. Because of her great loyalty to this work and the lineage, she agrees to the Priest's request. She goes back to her priestesses and quietly tells them that they must leave the Temple space to do their work outside. And they leave.

The High Priestess glances one last time at the maiden lying there in an altered state ready to receive. Satiated in her purity, fully surrendered, and fully open. She turns to the High Priest and exchanges a transmission that only they know about. The High Priest nods and escorts her to the door and closes it behind her.

The High Priestess gathers her priestesses together. They do their work and prayers to invoke and open the womb space to allow for this rite of passage, this sacred union to be birthed. There is an uneasiness within the circle of women. Many unanswered questions. Many concerned hearts as they stand on the precipice of an unknown horizon.

Inside the Temple, they hear abrupt movements and powerful chanting from the priests in an energy they haven't heard before. An invigorating energy. Strong, masculine, electrifying, resounding, and booming through the Temple. The vibration can be felt outside, and it causes a disturbance within the collective field of the priestesses.

The maiden, fully aligned with her faith, is breathing into the deepest places within her, realizing she hasn't been guided for this part. She wasn't told about this stage of the ritual, and so she trusts in the unknowable mystery of initiation and believes this must simply be part of it. She holds on to the deepest recesses of her belief.

The High Priest has been consumed by a great power. He feels guided and orchestrated to perform heiros gamos, the sacred union, himself. He feels it is his rightful duty to physically penetrate this young maiden, to act on behalf of God and make love to her in a mortal way.

The priests haven't been told about this. They witness what is happening to their master, and with their faith they tell themselves that even though it is unknowable and untold, somehow it must be right.

Lost in this ocean of incredible energy, everyone plays along with the unfolding of events. The High Priest thrusts himself upon the maiden. The maiden trusts that somehow this must be right. Otherwise, she wouldn't be here, this wouldn't be happening, right? This simply must be part of the awakening process.

The priests align with their High Priest supporting him, strengthening him with their prayers and their invocations. Outside the priestesses know what is going on. They know. They are so lost in their turmoil they cannot look at one another. They know what is going on, and a great wave of darkness comes into their hearts. The High Priest has been transformed into another aspect of his being and invites the other priests to also inseminate the maiden.

This energy is a free-for-all, a mélange of magic and incantation. There *are no words. It is a frenetic, chaotic quantum field of unique expressions. The priests are also aware that they are losing themselves, that they are being wrapped up in this chaotic field, as they continue to conjure up a great force inside of themselves and lose themselves to it.*

The young maiden continues to trust in the process.

The High Priestess is filled with an unspeakable regret, as the descent of such a great weight comes to her. She simply stands there trembling because she can see what is happening. And she is unable to stop it. She can see the young maiden's faith is unmoving, unyielding, and holding strong. She can see how the priests have become lost and fragmented, spiraling into chaos. And she can see the devastating arrival of distrust within the priestesses. She is seeing the whole moment for what it is. The Original Rape, on so many levels. The rape between women, the rape between men, the rape between men and women, and the rape between human and Divine. And she is seeing and feeling it all.

And she stands there with her arms open and palms flat, holding the posture of the Holy Mother, simply allowing this to be birthed through her. Allowing it to be. Allowing it to be on behalf of the young maiden, on behalf of the priestesses, on behalf of the priests, on behalf of the High Priest, on behalf of the lineage, on behalf of this unique and historical moment. Not knowing, not needing to know, but being acutely present. And she stands there in silence and so profoundly drenched in kindness as the downfall comes into full manifestation.

The priestesses have yet to glimpse this precipice that she is standing on. They have yet to reach this state of being, and they are crumbling. They are clawing their way toward this place, but it is not yet theirs. And so the regret and the distrust has its way with them, and they all run away in separate directions, knowing they will never see one another again. They simply cannot withstand or hold the birth. They simply have to leave, they cannot bear to see or listen with their inner senses to the scene that is happening inside of the Temple. It is only the High Priestess that can bear this. They run away and leave her.

The High Priestess knows that this is also going to happen to the priests.

She knows there will be a great devastation, a fragmentation of their lineage, a discombobulation, and a walking away to never, ever return.

The door opens, and the priests slowly walk out. Confused. Withdrawn. Shocked. Devastated by their actions. They do not look at the High Priestess. In a bleary daze, they walk off in separate directions never to be seen again.

The High Priest is last to leave. As he does, he looks at the High Priestess. And his eyes are flooded with sorrow, fright, and confusion. He is a swarm of emotions. He looks at her, and she looks at him. She remains standing from the deep place of stillness. She is not endorsing his actions; she is simply looking at him, she is witnessing him and what happened—fully and completely.

After what feels like forever, she utters five simple words: "Why did you do it?"

"Why did you let me?" he whispers and walks away never to be seen again.

As this transmission continues in ways that I could never be permitted to speak, know that the maiden is still there. Still lying on that altar, holding the space of the original purity and the remembrance of the true way.

Why Did You Do It?
Why Did You Let Me?

I believe "The Original Rape" transmission encapsulates where we currently stand. We are waking up to the current inner and outer world crisis, and we quite rightly want to shout and scream and demand answers. We are vexed and awake and want to know more of the truth. We stagger in disbelief now that the lid of Pandora's box has been lifted—and we are angry and fiercely so.

"The Original Rape" is a sickening story, a recognizable story, and a true story. It is the mythical story of the demise of the Temple. It maps the blow-by-blow account of how deceit, dishonor, and corruption began to contaminate the early priests and priestesses of our time. It's hard to pinpoint who did the dirty deed, as it's clear by the end of the story that the demise of the Temple was a collective agreement, made manifest by a group of people, not just one.

And this is where we are now.

Imagine that nauseating moment when your fellow priestesses realize what has happened and are so shocked by the events they cannot speak for fear of a fury they have never known. They stare in disbelief, hoping you, as High Priestess, will do something to make it all alright again. But you can't. The sacrilegious act has already happened. There is no going back now. In horror, their suspicions now realized, they scream out loud, "No!" and run away in wretched pain and disbelief.

The priests also flee, sick to their stomachs over what they have done. There is no temple anymore. It has been dirtied, ruined, smeared with wrongful actions. There is no reason to stay; they cannot look one another in the eye, let alone God.

Then imagine the moment when the High Priest comes out of the Temple, after he has hungrily fornicated with a young maiden pretending he was acting on behalf of God, and stands before you, the beginnings of shame in his eyes. As the High Priestess, you can smell the deceit and the debauchery, you know something is very, very wrong, but because it has never happened before, you foolishly refuse to question yourself. You cannot imagine that this man, whom you have known and loved forever as your brother, friend, and confidant, would ever betray the faith or the Temple, and yet, he clearly has, but you dare not think how, or why. And so he stands there, head slightly hanging, hoping to avoid what must come next.

Your heart is pounding and your throat parched, as you ask, "Why did you do it?"

And he replies, "Why did you let me?"

The question, "Why did you let me?" must not only reach our ears, but beckon forth a worthy answer. It has to shatter everything. It has to obliterate every reason, excuse, justification, and complaint. It has to obliterate every "poor me," "betrayed me," and "vengeful me" storyline. Everything. It has to render us dumbfounded as the horribly honest, clear realization begins to dawn on us. We are giving this death machine the power it needs to fulfill its enslavement of us. We, us, you, and me. It's so simple that we immediately discard it. But don't. Don't go there. Wait, just a moment. Let it percolate and circulate. What if we are the ones keeping this warped reality in place? Could it actually be that the moment we say no is the moment it begins to change?

Blind compassion is rooted in the belief that we are all doing the best we can, and we are not. We are cutting ourselves and everyone else far too much slack. We are not at optimum potential, but we pretend to be. Our game playing is costing lives—the lives of others and our own. We must no longer care about coming across as a "good" or "spiritual" person. Our fiery anger must be shown when we stand our ground and protect our innocence. An unrelentingly positive expression is not the answer and neither is fearmongering. An unknown third option is appearing on the horizon. It's called Truth. Not something that is spoken, but something that is lived.

Anger is not aggression. Forcefulness is not violence. Discernment is not judgment. Love is not weak.

Pause here for reflection. Take the time that is needed to truly be with these insights and understandings. Just breathe and be with them. Let's bear witness to the sobriety of the situation and feel one another as we rise together to receive more of Her transmission.

Let's move on without answers.

We must learn to trust the process, remembering that *this is an initiation.*

Initiation

You'll be initiated,
when you are ready.

Life knows,
and the initiation rites
are waiting.

Where you are holding,
you will be broken.

Where you've lost heart,
you will be shaken.

Where you are careless,
you'll meet your neglect.

What you are averse to
will be total and stark.

What you are attached to
will be pried from your grips.

Ignorance will be
wrought with vision,
a burning,
to make you see.

You are loved so much
that you will be engulfed in
the flames
of love's fire,
in order to
ignite your own
heart's flames,
and fulfill love's destiny.

Alchemical change will ensue,
destroying you,
to make way for
new love.

Licked by some Hellish ordeal,
Ambivalence gives way to Engagement,
Rage engenders Clarity,
Anxiety becomes Inspiration,
Apathy roars into Feeling,
Melancholy imbues its Depth,
Licked by some Heavenly delight.

Phoenixed, you'll fly,
the hero of your own journey,
wielding revelatory fire,
with great Wisdom
and Compassion,
a Gestalt,
anew.

The circle closes,
it is a spiral,
to the beginning,
of another
Circle.

CHRISTOPHER WALLACE

The overall point of this book is to take personal
and collective responsibility.

Index